NEW FOUNDATIONS THEOLOGICAL LIBRARY

General Editor
PETER TOON, MA, M.TH, D.PHIL

Consultant Editor
RALPH P. MARTIN, MA, PH.D

NEW FOUNDATIONS THEOLOGICAL LIBRARY

Other volumes in preparation

HOLINESS
AND THE
WILL OF GOD

*Perspectives on the
Theology of Tertullian*

GERALD LEWIS BRAY

JOHN KNOX PRESS

ATLANTA

Library of Congress Cataloging in Publication Data

Bray, Gerald Lewis.
  Holiness and the will of God.

  (New foundations theological library)
  'List of Tertullian's works': p. 169
  Bibliography: p. 171
  Includes index.
    1. Tertullianus, Quintus Septimus Florens.
  1. Title.
  BR65.T7B754   1979   230'.1'30924   79-5211
  ISBN 0-8042-3705-0

Published simultaneously by Marshall, Morgan & Scott in Great Britain and by John Knox Press in the United States of America, 1979.

John Knox Press
Atlanta

Printed in Great Britain

CONTENTS

PREFACE

The present book is an attempt to reflect seriously on Tertullian's theology and its implications for Christian faith. It appears at a moment when the patristic writers are being increasingly attacked for having allowed their own intellectual and cultural presuppositions to penetrate and distort their spiritual understanding. It is perhaps too much to say that a good deal of current debate on the subject is ill-informed, but it is certainly true that it is often poorly documented, and that a contrary opinion is by no means excluded by the evidence. Sweeping judgments of the ancients are always dangerous, especially when they are made by scholars whose own position is fundamentally unsympathetic.

No one would question the fact that circumstances often exert considerable influence on even the most detached of writers, though it is perhaps less frequently realised that this particular limitation was not the exclusive preserve of the early Christians. The interaction of faith and culture during the first Christian centuries however is of particular interest, in that it was this period which witnessed the rise of the basic framework of classical dogmatic theology. The accusation that cultural relativism conditioned this development is almost always accompanied by an express desire to abandon traditional doctrines in favour of a radical reappraisal of Christian belief in which distinctions implied by a word like 'orthodoxy' would disappear.

In his *Method in Theology* Bernard Lonergan says that ancient structures of thought postulated the existence of absolute principles and values to which true human culture aspired. This objective approach, which Lonergan calls classicism, is no longer tenable in the light of modern theories of relativity. As Lonergan explains it, each culture has norms which are valid within its context, but which lose their relevance once this context is transcended or destroyed. It was the mistake of traditional Christianity to assume that Graeco-Roman culture was the universal norm, and that theological statements made within that culture had an eternal validity.

At first sight, Lonergan's thesis is very attractive, especially since it is undoubtedly true that the early Christians were products of a universalist education and could hardly escape the mental climate of the Roman world-empire. But true though this is, it is fatally easy to exaggerate the influence of such factors on the patristic writers. Almost from the beginning Christianity suffered persecution from the imperial authorities, and no Christian could fail to realise that his religion was diametrically opposed to the established order. Moreover, the substance of the faith came into the Graeco-Roman world from an essentially foreign milieu, and Hebraic notions of God were always held to be superior to their pagan counterparts, even by those writers who were most anxious to reconcile them as far as possible.

The concept of orthodoxy may be related to classical ideals, but this relationship does not depend on the influence of pagan philosophy. Christianity was radically different in that its doctrines were based on divine revelation rather than on human speculation. The normative character of the Scriptures as the Word of God made all the difference. However much the Fathers of the Church may have misinterpreted the Word in particular instances, they never lost sight of its objective character as the Christian's final authority in matters of faith. Their conviction that Scriptural revelation was the sum of all wisdom gave them a weapon which ultimately enabled them to conquer the whole of ancient thought.

It is a great pity that the study of this process in recent years has been marked by a tendency to underestimate the power of Christianity to convert the minds of men. Hardly any of the great thinkers of the first few centuries came from a Christian home; none lived in an environment in which Christianity was taken for granted. Whatever inducement there may have been to accept the new faith was more than offset by social and political pressures against it. In such an atmosphere it is inconceivable that a religion as strange to the Hellenistic mind as Christianity could have prospered, unless it had something to offer men which no other creed had. Christianity stands out in antiquity not because it successfully married Jewish with

Hellenistic insights into God, but because it offered a faith more profound and more deeply satisfying than either of these.

To the Fathers of the Church, Christian theology was the work of the converted mind seeking to get to grips with the teaching of Scripture. Compared with ancient philosophy, it contains little in the way of speculation, and even less diversity of approach. However different Antiochenes and Alexandrians, Apologists and Cappadocians may appear to us, to their non-Christian contemporaries they spoke as one voice. Later generations drew upon the work of earlier ones not as imperfect specimens of theological activity which required substantial revision in the light of subsequent reflection, but as models to be revered and imitated, even as they were expanded and developed further.

The position adopted in this book is that the early Christians must be allowed to speak as far as possible on their own terms. What presuppositions did an ancient writer bring to Christianity and how did these change when he was converted? What principles guided him as he sought to construct a theology? Are these principles still valid today? These are the questions we must bear in mind in our approach to the study of Tertullian.

Tertullian (*fl. circa* 195–212) is not an obvious choice in some ways, since his writings have always been controversial, and there are other ancient theologians whose work may be reckoned to have been of greater historical importance. But although there are certainly disadvantages to be overcome, a study of his writings will also yield us important benefits. For one thing, he is one of the few ancient Christian writers whose works survive almost intact, and who wrote with equal conviction against heretics on abstruse points of doctrine and against deviants at the most popular level. In his treatises we meet the entire range of ecclesiastical life, which gives them a fullness often lacking in the more cerebral essays of other writers. We are therefore in a much better position to probe his cultural background and test the extent to which it influenced his thought.

A few remarks about the format of the work may be helpful to the reader. Quotations from French and German writers are given in English in the text, but in cases where there is no printed English translation available, the original is given in the notes. Latin quotations appear in full, with an English translation following in the text. In cases where the argument depends on the actual words of the Greek or Latin, and not on the general sense of the text, no translation has been given. Notes have been collected at the end.

It remains for me to thank all those who have helped in seeing this book on its way to publication. First, I must express my gratitude to the Master and Fellows of Trinity College, whose generosity enabled me to begin my research, and to the Tyndale Fellowship for Biblical Research, in whose excellent library the work was brought to completion. I am also indebted to the Reverend Professor C. F. D. Moule, who so freely offered his assistance at various points, and to Mr David Wright, who read the manuscript and offered many valuable comments and corrections. My thanks are due also to Andrew Gandon, who in the name of friendship stretched his great resources of patience to correct and improve the style of the text. To these and to many others who have helped in various ways I am most deeply grateful.

Scribebam Cantabrigiae
ad festam Pentecostes
A.S. MCMLXXVIII

CHAPTER ONE

PAST AND PRESENT

In the long history of the Western Church, there can be few figures who have been the object of such enduring fascination as Tertullian. For centuries churchmen and lay scholars have pondered the writings of this trenchant yet elusive controversialist, and discussed whether they are orthodox, heretical, a bit of both or somewhere in between. Has his influence on the Church been harmful or beneficial, or have the two tendencies cancelled one another out? The question has seldom received a clearcut answer, and certainly none which has ever proved to be definitive. Then as now, Tertullian has been a borderline figure, neither officially recognised as a saint nor explicitly condemned as a heretic. In the East, apart from a few brief references in Eusebius,[1] Tertullian has been very largely ignored – the fate of anyone who chose to write in Latin. But in the West, his influence has left an indelible mark on the history of the Church. It is certainly true that he has not been adulated like the great luminaries of the fourth century, but leaving aside the issue of his orthodoxy, the comparison is surely unfair. For if both Jerome and Augustine can point to an impressive following down the centuries, we must remember that it was their intention, after all, to give the Church a cultural and intellectual foundation which would stand the test of time. Furthermore, their labours were always widely supported, and not only by the Church; the State and the social climate in general were on their side. The difficulties and opposition which they did encounter seem insignificant in comparison with the troubles which afflicted the whole Church in the centuries of persecution. From the moment they began to write, both Jerome and Augustine enjoyed an audience which (in the West at any rate) was universal. Equally important, they had the benefit of a large number of illustrious predecessors, both Greek and Latin, whose ideas they could borrow and whose mistakes they could avoid. All these advantages were denied

Tertullian. It was his lot to blaze trails for others to follow, and we must not blame him too severely if succeeding generations sometimes found firmer ground to tread on.

Tertullian lived in an age which, in spite of all its enlightenment, remained curiously frightened and consequently intolerant of that inexplicable religious novelty men called Christianity. He knew only too well how ludicrously unjust was the persecution meted out to Christians, but he also knew that prejudice had dulled the wits of otherwise sensible men, and that their blindness was invincible. At times we get an impression in his writings of a deeper malaise. The late second century was a time of growing insecurity, characterised by a loss of faith in the traditional values of Hellenism. The classical virtues of justice and reason, to which Tertullian appealed in his defence of the Christians, were fighting a losing battle against this rising current of doubt and anxiety. Christians did well to tremble at the news of fresh disaster. In a society beset with fears for its very existence, they appeared as a subversive element which eagerly awaited the prospect of imminent collapse. Such people were unlikely to be spared the wrath of a mob determined to vent its frustration on the first available victim. Tertullian paints the scene vividly, and even when allowance is made for rhetorical flourish, the picture is grim enough (see, e.g., *Apol.* 40. 1–2). In these circumstances it is surprising that Tertullian was able to write at all. Yet when we remember that it was he more than anyone who captured the world of Latin letters for the faith of Christ, we may begin to appreciate how great and how lasting his achievement was.

His extant works are thirty-one in number, and these will easily fill two large volumes. No other Latin Christian writer from the age of persecution has left us anything like as much, and we must remember that the surviving texts may represent as little as half the total number of his compositions. We know that some of his treatises were written in Greek, but these no longer survive. There are also a number of works to which his name has been attached, but which, in the opinion of most scholars, are unauthentic. These include a stirring account of the martyrdom of Perpetua and Felicity, which occurred in AD 203, a short treatise against heresies, and a poem attacking the heretic Marcion.

But even if we leave these aside, the extent and range of the surviving corpus is still remarkable. Lack of sufficient information makes it impossible to say for certain how long Tertullian's literary career lasted, but the bulk of his writings seem to be datable to the reigns of the African emperor Septimius Severus (AD 193–211) and of his son Caracalla (AD 211–17). It therefore seems likely that he must have written on average two books a year, a considerable achievement even in an age when a 'book' was often little more than a short pamphlet. These books may be divided according to content into five broad categories, two of which may then be further subdivided in line with Tertullian's special interests.

The first, and in some ways most appealing of these, is apologetic. Its most substantial representative is a lengthy treatise called simply *Apologeticum*, which is now extant in two separate recensions. Closely related to it is an earlier work *Ad nationes*, of which *Apologeticum* was probably a later expansion. In these books Tertullian undertakes a thorough-going defence of Christians in the face of pagan prejudice and persecution. He points out that the popular belief that Christians were members of an immoral secret society, bent on the destruction of the Empire, has no basis in fact, and goes on to argue for the reasonableness and historical certainty of Christian truth as opposed to the irrationality of paganism. His emphasis is everywhere on people and events rather than on theories and doctrines, and it is this which continues to give *Apologeticum* a wide popular appeal. As a source-book for early Christian life and attitudes it is invaluable, though some of the factual details it records may have suffered distortion in the course of argument.

Two smaller works in a similar vein are a short treatise on the testimony of the soul (*De testimonio animae*), which outlines Tertullian's belief that the natural man is subconsciously aware of Christian truth despite his outward profession of paganism, and a rhetorical address to Scapula, Roman governor of Africa in AD 212, in which he argues against the legal disabilities imposed on Christians.

A second category of works takes up the theme of persecution and deals with it from the standpoint of the confessing Christian. Tertullian stresses the virtues of fortitude and exhorts the martyrs to die a death worthy of their faith. At times he leaves the impression of vacillation on certain points, particularly on the validity of flight in persecution. Sometimes he allows for this and advises on the conduct proper to a refugee, but we must remember that elsewhere he explicitly condemns it in a special treatise devoted to the subject (*De fuga in persecutione*). The general impression is that whilst he may have accepted such realities when they did not impinge on the main issue under discussion, his own sympathies inclined him towards an unrelenting rigorism in the face of the ultimate test of a Christian's religious sincerity.

Next comes a series of tracts dealing with various aspects of Christian piety and practice. There are short treatises on prayer (*De oratione*), fasting (*De ieiunio*), long-suffering (*De patientia*) and repentance (*De paenitentia*). These are chiefly of interest for the line they take – or seem to take – on such matters as the possibility of forgiveness for sins committed after baptism. This is another subject where Tertullian is inconsistent, though once again it is largely a question of priorities. As with flight in persecution, Tertullian shows a remarkable ability to insist on the strictest possible discipline in principle, and yet adjust it under the pressure of circumstances to the point where he almost ignores it completely. Scholars usually explain these discrepancies in his teaching by assigning the more tolerant passages to an early stage of his career, before he came into contact with the extremism of the Montanists. Such a theory is plausible, but unnecessary. Tertullian's examples of tolerance are all circumstantial and deal with actual cases, whilst his doctrinaire attitudes normally come out only when he is stating a general principle. May it not be that with him, as with so many others, theoretical justice was tempered with practical mercy, without any consciousness of these two things being fundamentally incompatible?

Of particular importance is his work on baptism (*De baptismo*) in which he examines the sacrament at length. It seems that many people were questioning the need for such a rite, and Tertullian goes into great detail about the purifying effects of consecrated water on sinful human flesh. To us his language sounds almost magical, but we should remember that his main concern was to counter a spiritualising tendency which degraded the material world and put it outside the sphere of redemption. In his treatise Tertullian criticises the widespread practice of infant baptism, on the ground that it fails to take account of a child's propensity to sin without knowing it. For in Tertullian's theology of baptism, a baptised child who committed a sin, even without knowing it, would lose his eternal salvation, unless he could redeem himself by the blood of martyrdom.

Also in this category was a work on ecstasy (*De extasi*), which is unfortunately no longer extant. Tertullian makes casual allusions to ecstatic activity in other treatises, and these have often been advanced as evidence that he shared a 'charismatic' kind of piety. The loss of *De extasi* is therefore a matter of some regret, as it would probably have enabled us to view this whole question in greater perspective. As it is, we know that he was certainly well-disposed towards those who had had unusual spiritual experiences, even when these bordered on the paranormal, but we cannot say for certain whether or to what extent he participated in such activity himself. There is no doubt that he accepted such things as necessary in the life of the *Church*, but there is no evidence to indicate that he regarded them as mandatory for, or usual among individual believers.

The fourth category of his writings, which may be subdivided into two, concerns the individual Christian's piety in relation to the surrounding world. Some of these writings deal with general subjects like public entertainments (*De spectaculis*), idolatry (*De idololatria*), and the crown which soldiers wore to celebrate victories and special imperial favours (*De corona*). The greater number, however, are concerned with the place of women in the Church. Tertullian was preoccupied with this subject to the point of obsession, and returned to it whenever he could. He exhorted Christian women to live modestly, particularly in matters of dress and adornment, and ruled out the possibility of second marriages in this life. He regarded sexual intercourse as sinful and encouraged believers to forgo the joys of parenthood on the ground that Christ would soon return and bring the world to an end. Marriage he tolerated, in line with biblical teaching, but it was to be a purely spiritual affair. It is odd, though extremely significant, that this lack of enthusiasm for marriage and procreation was in spite of his general tendency to exalt the created world as a gift of a beneficent God.

The fifth and last major category is doctrinal. This too, may be subdivided, according to whether a particular work is positive or negative in intention. The treatises with a positive bent deal mostly with the nature of man and the incarnation of Christ. The most important of them, and the most intellectual of all Tertullian's writings, is *De anima*, which presents a Christian critique of various philosophical ideas concerning the nature of the human soul. In it he argues against the Platonists' doctrine of the soul's incorporeality, and favours the Stoic teaching instead. For this reason he has sometimes been called a 'materialist', though to say this is to misunderstand his use of the term 'body'. For Tertullian a 'body' was not necessarily material in substance, and much of *De anima* is taken up with what amounts in effect to a refutation of this assumption. Of all Tertullian's treatises, *De anima* is the one which is most unjustly neglected today, in spite of a masterly edition of it by Jan Waszink (Amsterdam, 1947).

The union of spirit and matter forms the underlying theme of two other works, both of them substantial. *De carne Christi* asserts the reality of the incarnation, and may fairly be claimed to be Chalcedonian *avant la lettre*, while its sequel, *De resurrectione carnis* (or *mortuorum*) examines in detail what is meant by the resurrection of the flesh. All these treatises display a wealth of biological knowledge unusual in a theologian, and it is remarkable how little in them seems dated, even to a modern reader.

On the negative side are Tertullian's numerous treatises against heretics of various kinds. He was at great pains to condemn the dualism of Hermogenes, who apparently believed that matter was evil, and also the fanciful speculations of the Valentinians, who constructed a hierarchy of supernatural beings out of such abstract terms as Wisdom, Fullness (*Pleroma*) and Mind (*Nous*). His main attack, however, was reserved for Marcion, a trader from the Black Sea who had tried to downgrade the Old Testament and had so purged the New as to leave almost nothing but Luke's Gospel and the Pauline Epistles. In answering him, Tertullian took five books, in which he demonstrated how even Marcion's reduced canon could not be understood without the Old Testament, and how true Christian faith involved an integrated world-view in which the same God was both Creator and Redeemer.

But the most famous anti-heretical treatise of all is undoubtedly the one against Praxeas, an unknown Greek who claimed that Father, Son and Holy Spirit were but names to distinguish the different operations of the one God. This teaching, which in Tertullian's phrase, 'crucified the Father', led him to develop the first full-length doctrine of the Trinity. To a later generation it appears to have traces of subordinationism (the belief that the Son and the Spirit are inferior to the Father), but in the context of its time it is a triumphant statement of orthodoxy, and one which can still provoke debate today.

Also in this category is a long study of heresy in the abstract. *De praescriptione haereticorum* is an attempt to isolate the root cause of heresy and to guard against it. Much of Tertullian's argument concerns the interpretation of Scripture, which he insists must be read as an organic whole within the context of the (apostolic) Rule of Faith. This argument is unlikely to sound very convincing to a modern reader, but it is of great interest for the light which it sheds on the state of Christian doctrine around the year 200.

Tertullian also wrote against the Jews (*Adversus Iudaeos*), though the text of this work is clearly composite. Probably some of it comes from other hands, though we cannot be sure whether Tertullian reworked existing material or whether others edited an unfinished work of his.

When discussing Tertullian's polemical works, it is only fair to remember that he seldom if ever indulged in personal attacks or backbiting of the kind so frequent in writers like Jerome. Certainly he had harsh things to say about certain individuals, but their offence was invariably against Christian truth, not against him personally. Furthermore, the only people he condemned by name were heretics whom the Church had already condemned; when this was not the case, he tended to resort to anonymity. Thus his harsh criticism of the 'bishop of bishops' (*De pud.* 20.21) leaves us guessing his identity, and even his see, which may have been Rome or (as Barnes thinks) Carthage. The only possible exception to this rule is Praxeas, but it is far from certain that this was his real name, since it could well be a Greek nickname meaning 'busybody'.

Outside all categories is the last and most enigmatic of Tertullian's writings, *De pallio*. This is a tongue-in-cheek study of ancient habits of dress, in which the noble Roman toga is compared unfavourably with the pallium of the Greek philosophers. Many Romans were taking to the latter as a sign of learning, though it was also popular with the Christians, and would a cautious Roman risk being associated with such disreputable people? *De pallio* stands out as an oddity, so much so that some have even claimed that it antedates Tertullian's conversion. This, however, is unlikely. Like so much else in his writings, *De pallio* proves nothing but that he was a great thinker and writer, capable of unusual versatility and gifted with a somewhat untheological sense of humour.

Tertullian's achievement as a writer was immense. His wide-ranging doctrinal studies offered valuable ammunition to the Christians, and enabled them to take the offensive at all levels of ancient society. Tertullian put Christianity on the cultural map in a way which it had never been before, and his writings were the staple diet of Latin Christianity until at least the fourth century. As a moralist, he strikes us as puritanical, but this must be seen in perspective. Most early Christian writers had leanings towards asceticism, and Tertullian is sweet reasonableness when set alongside Jerome, or the Desert Fathers. Even after he fell victim to the charge of heresy, his writings were too valuable to be burned, and that in itself is a tribute to his lasting greatness as a Christian theologian and apologist.

TERTULLIAN IN CHRISTIAN TRADITION

For centuries the critical study of Tertullian's works, such as it was, was the exclusive preserve of the Church. In the age of persecution, however, there was no time to spare in which to write a biography of a controversial figure who to all appearances was not even a martyr, with the result that contemporary records are blank. Tertullian himself never dwelt on autobiographical details, and there is remarkably little which can be deduced with certainty from his writings, despite long and acrimonious controversies, many of them quite fruitless, which have raged over various 'clues' which they have been supposed to provide. In the end all we can really say about Tertullian's life is that we know virtually nothing about it, and whatever mark he may have left on his own time and society has escaped the notice of posterity.

On the whole, Tertullian's works have survived not because of the secular achievements of their author, but because their intrinsic merit and interest has earned them a place in Christian tradition. It was their theological value (despite the taint of heresy) and not their literary worth which ensured their survival. The Ciceronian revival which permeated Latin letters in the fourth century ensured that Tertullian's reputation as a classicist was never very high. Even a Christian writer like Lactantius (*Inst. div.* v.1.3) felt free to disapprove of his style, and had it not been for the subsequent triumph of Christianity his fame would almost certainly have gone the way of many another second-century rhetorician, his talent unsung by a forgetful posterity.

Tertullian ostensibly wrote many of his works, and especially the famous *Apologeticum*, for a largely pagan audience whom he hoped to reach with the Gospel. Whatever success he may have had in this attempt has escaped the notice of history, but there is no doubt that from a very early date his writings were required reading in the North African Church. Cyprian, who was bishop of Carthage a generation or so after Tertullian's death, apparently read the 'master' every day, if Jerome (*De vir. ill.* 53) can be believed. His writings certainly betray a considerable indebtedness to those of his illustrious predecessor, and the same may be said of Novatian and even of his critic Lactantius.[2]

It was not until Tertullian was being widely read and imitated in the Western Church that doubts concerning his orthodoxy began to be expressed. Hilary of Poitiers, for example, remarks on the excellence of Tertullian's commentary on the Beatitudes (now lost), adding however that its authority was lessened by the author's subsequent lapse into heresy.[3] Jerome is more precise – he claims that Tertullian became a Montanist in middle age, but puts the blame for this squarely on the envy and insults of the Roman clergy.[4] This sympathetic attitude had worn thin by the end of the fourth century, however, and Tertullian's writings were no longer read and copied with the same interest as before.

We cannot now retrace in detail the steps which led to the final condemnation of Tertullian's works at the end of the fifth century, though no doubt one important factor was the use which dissident movements had been able to make of them. Indeed, it may well have been schisms in the North African Church which brought him under suspicion of heresy in the first place. It is generally thought that the reluctance of early writers to mention him by name is evidence that they regarded him as a heretic from whom they wished to dissociate themselves as much as possible, but this is by no means obvious. It was not unusual to borrow from earlier writers without mentioning their names; Tertullian himself made veiled references to other Christian authors, and he certainly did not regard them as heretical.[5] It is also difficult to imagine how, if this were indeed the case, an impeccably orthodox Churchman like Cyprian could have esteemed him as highly as he did – 'master' is not the sort of word Cyprian would have reserved for someone who was a notorious schismatic. It is also somewhat surprising that Eusebius betrays no knowledge of the fact. Surely it cannot be coincidence that clear references to Tertullian's heresy begin to appear only after the disruption in the North African Church caused by the Donatist schism. This suspicion is strengthened by Augustine, who mentions Tertullian's heresy in connection with the sect of the Tertullianistae, a small body which he helped to reintegrate into the Catholic Church. According to Augustine, the sect was a lingering survival of a dissenting movement led by Tertullian himself, but although this may have been sincerely believed on both sides, it is on balance unlikely. More probably the Tertullianistae came into being early in the fourth century. In the charged atmosphere of the time, when the members of the African Church had to choose between a newly legalised, semi-official Christianity and the stricter traditions of the ancient brotherhood of martyrs, what could have been more natural than for a small group to declare its loyalty to the greatest figure their Church had produced, and to seek to rally men to his teachings as the authentic way of faith? Certainly the ease with which they were later

reincorporated into the Great Church makes it highly unlikely that they were Montanists in any recognisable sense.
Tertullian's writings became controversial at the very
moment when his works were more widely circulated and more
generally read than ever before. The objection made was not
that they taught false doctrine – Augustine was at pains to
point out that they did not[6] – but that they portrayed the
Church as an exclusive body of saints which rejected any kind
of compromise with the world. This was a conception which
appealed to the Donatists and their sympathisers, but which
was fundamentally out of tune with a Church which was
rapidly acquiring a religious monopoly within the Empire, and
which was accordingly obliged to widen its horizons (or lower
its standards, depending on the point of view). In such a
climate, the man who had exalted martyrdom as the norm for
Christians, and who had backed dissident minorities against
central authority, could not escape censure. Perhaps it was in
this way that Tertullian's fate was finally sealed.

All the same, condemnation was slow in coming and seems
not to have been very effective. Writing against the Donatists,
Optatus of Milevis (*De sch. Don.* i. 9) was able to claim
Tertullian's support, and it was not until the publication of the
famous *Decretum de libris recipiendis et non recipiendis*, attributed,
probably erroneously, to Pope Gelasius I (d. 496), that his
writings were finally proscribed. But even in the sixth century
he was still being mentioned, evidently with approval, by
Isidore of Seville (*Chron.* 81). After Isidore's time, however,
Tertullian drops out of sight. The triumph of Augustinianism
was not favourable to him, and his writings contained little of
value which by that time could not be found elsewhere. Portions
of his writings were still copied from time to time, and the
extant manuscript tradition can be traced to the ninth century.
General interest in Tertullian, however, seems to have revived
in the late Middle Ages – there are no fewer than twenty
manuscripts from the fifteenth century – after an apparent gap
of three hundred years. This renewed interest coincided with
the religious ferment building up in Europe at this period, and
the violence of Tertullian's anti-Roman polemic came into its
own at the Reformation. As the structure of the mediaeval
Church was shaken to its foundations, the writings of the early

Fathers took on a new importance. Protestants naturally found his invective against the Roman establishment a veritable god-send, although his brilliance and wit found admirers among the adherents of the old religion too – notably Jacques Bossuet.

The Reformation, however, did not alter the traditional picture of Tertullian given by Jerome and Augustine. In fact, churchmen of the sixteenth and seventeenth centuries were as ambiguous in their appreciation of his genius as their fourth-century predecessors had been. Antiquarians though they were almost to a man, their interest in Tertullian was not historical in the modern sense. The Early Church period was of interest to them because it bore direct relevance to their own age and its problems. Tertullian was important chiefly because he could be quoted as an authoritative witness in the debate about papal claims or the sacraments. These debates seem remote from us now, but their legacy still casts its shadow over academic study. Scholars still speak, for instance, of Tertullian's 'Catholic' period, with more than a hint that there was a time in his career when his pen was unquestioningly at the service of the Pope in the defence of post-Tridentine dogma. The decrees of the First Vatican Council (1870) and the subsequent strenuous efforts of Rome to counteract the effects of modern scholarship have kept alive the traditional picture of Tertullian, the priest gone wrong. Even as reputable a scholar as the late Cardinal Daniélou, in a review of T. D. Barnes' book, expressed surprise that Barnes should have made Tertullian seem more like a parson than a curé, so difficult was it for him to escape the clerical image.[7] At a more fundamental level, the basic differences between Protestantism and post-Tridentine Catholicism have produced two separate traditions of scholarship, a fact of major importance in the development of modern research.

But despite all the efforts, of Rome in particular, to counteract modern thought, there can be no doubt that the traditional Christian view of Tertullian no longer dominates the academic scene. It still survives of course in those manuals of devotion written by non-specialists for the edification of the unlearned, and it is occasionally found in polemical works which like to quote his opinion on baptism, or the gifts of the Spirit. But on the whole, the traditional view of his work no longer carries weight in scholarly circles. The secularisation of Western culture has produced a generation with a different mind, and another set of questions. It is to these questions and the outlook behind them that we must now turn our attention.

SECULARISATION AND ITS EFFECTS

By the late seventeenth century, the wars of religion had ended, and the general climate of theological reaction had set the stage between the Protestant freethinkers and the Platonic humanism which the Reformation had temporarily eclipsed. The new rationalists, however, were not on the whole atheists. Most of them clung to a nominal Christianity and attempted to secure intellectual independence by positing that faith and reason were distinct though not incompatible modes of thought. In their scheme of things rational logic could lead a man to Christian faith as surely – nay, more surely – than humble acceptance of Divine Revelation. For Revelation, as found in Scripture, had necessarily been obliged to accommodate itself to the age of ignorance, with its superstitious cast of mind. To them evil spirits, miracles, indeed anything that was supernatural, represented an alien accretion to the primitive faith of mankind. The new age of 'enlightenment' had begun.

As a counterweight to rationalism there emerged an emotionally powerful para-ecclesiastical Pietism, which by 1750 was becoming a major religious force throughout Protestant Europe. The pietists were not ignorant men, nor were they indifferent to Christian doctrine – Wesley, for example, spent a good deal of energy attacking the Calvinist teaching on predestination – but the heart of their religion lay in religious experience. As long as a man knew what it was to be 'born again', the niceties of doctrinal definition could be put to one side. The readiness of pietists to soft-pedal dogmatic questions was the key to the later alliance between them and the rationalists of the Enlightenment, and this has been a major factor in the growth of modern biblical and patristic scholarship.

David Hume helped this process forward by pointing out that there was nothing in the universe which made the chain of cause and effect necessary; he maintained that logical patterns were the result of observational habit, and depended on psychological factors found only in man himself.[8] Hume was certainly not a pietist, but he opened the way for man's non-rational faculties to play a role in philosophical speculation.

Rousseau took up Hume's challenge and was followed by Kant. Kant was acquainted with Pietism and saw that it made a powerful appeal to the emotions, although his rationalistic bias made him unsympathetic to its base in supernatural religion. To Kant, the passions, the spirit and the moral sense in man could all be explained as natural phenomena, without reference to God. He took over Hume's empiricism and added to it an integrated moral and spiritual dimension. In his system the human mind was the focus on which all man's faculties and impulses converged. The human mind was itself a microcosm of the supreme mind which, for those so inclined, could be called 'God'. Thus a knowledge of the microcosmic self was the key to a knowledge of God. He thus effectively removed any need for Christianity and prepared the way for a synthesis of Pietism and rationalism on a secular, rather than on a Christian, foundation.

It was Friedrich Schleiermacher who first realised the danger Kant's philosophy contained for the Church, and who tried to counter its subversive effects with a theory of his own. He accepted Kant's epistemological method but argued that the religious element in human life, far from being a primitive substitute for rationalism, was the supreme expression of man's moral and spiritual instincts. Wherever there was religion this truth could be detected, even if it was coated with a layer of corruption which obscured the essence. It was Christianity, argued Schleiermacher, which had achieved the highest expression of man's nature. He admitted that it too had suffered corruption in its development, but despite everything, Christianity, in its German and Protestant form, was the highest form of religion which had *evolved* up to then. In a very real sense Schleiermacher completed the marriage between Pietism and rationalism on a humanistic foundation, and the fruits of this union have dominated theological studies ever since.

FROM NEANDER TO HARNACK

At first it seemed as if Schleiermacher's ideas would be stillborn. Rationalists like Goethe rejected them out of hand[9] and the pietists were not interested. For a time they passed into oblivion, only to reappear suddenly in the writings of one of Schleiermacher's pupils, August Neander. Neander had been born a Jew, but converted to Christianity while still a youth. As a theological student in Halle, he attended Schleiermacher's lectures and was deeply impressed by the strength of his master's attacks on godless rationalism, a subject which greatly preoccupied him at the time. As a result of this, Neander came to believe that Christian history was the struggle for spiritual freedom against the chains of legalism and philosophy. While still a student, he determined to prove his thesis by a detailed study of the Church's history. Neander realised that the early centuries were of crucial importance for this, as it was against the familiar background of scepticism and rationalistic deism that Christianity spread across the Roman world. Neander emphasised the parallels between the Early Church period and the Germany of his own day, in order to demonstrate that Christianity could overcome modern atheism as successfully as it had defeated its ancient equivalent. As a prelude to this great history, Neander resolved to concentrate his attention on certain individuals whose lives seemed to him to exemplify in miniature the struggle of the whole Church. Interestingly enough, the first man he chose to study was Tertullian.

The appearance of *Antignosticus, Geist des Tertullians* in 1825 may fairly be said to mark the beginning of modern scholarly work on Tertullian. Much of the book was unexceptional, even traditional in tone. Following the canons laid down by Scholasticism, Neander divided the works into polemical, disciplinary and dogmatic treatises. Within each of these categories there was a further subdivision of works belonging to the 'pre-Montanist' and the 'Montanist' phases of his career. Neander's historical outlook was conservative, tending to follow the received opinions of ancient and renaissance commentators. Had his research gone no further, his book would have attracted little attention. But, of course, the traditional framework which Neander adopted was secondary to his real aims. Having been convinced by Schleiermacher that it was a man's personality and feelings which determined his outlook in matters of religion, Neander gave full weight to this aspect of Tertullian's character. Thus his lapse into Montanism was explained in terms of a rigorous and uncompromising temperament rather than as the outcome of an ecclesiastical or doctrinal dispute. As Neander says:

> Of Tertullian it especially holds good that he can be understood only from within – that we must possess a mental consanguinity with the spirit which dwelt in him, in order to recognize in the defective form, that higher quality which it contains, and to set it free from that confined form, which is always the business of genuine historical composition ... Tertullian, in the later part of his life, joined the sect of Montanus. As we have already remarked, it has been attempted, very erroneously, to explain this change by outward causes, instead of accounting for it by an internal congeniality of mind. If we go through his writings according to the various subjects of which they treat, the relation of the earlier writings of Tertullian to those in which he advocates Montanistic views, will be most clearly exhibited.[10]

In some respects Neander was a much more orthodox Christian than Schleiermacher had been. In particular he contended that Christianity was a unique phenomenon, not to be explained away by a theory of religious evolution. But at the same time he also championed the view that there was a sharp division between the New Testament period and later centuries, in which the Church lost its early perfection and became increasingly worldly and corrupt. According to Neander, things were so bad in the second century that even churchmen were accommodating the Faith to the prevailing rationalism of the day – an obvious parallel with contemporary Germany. It was this tendency which lay at the root of 'gnosticism', a vague concept to which Neander imparted new form and substance.[11] According to him, Tertullian was a spiritually minded Christian in the apostolic tradition who, seeing the danger to the Church, devoted his life to the fight for spiritual purity. Unfortunately an inherent bias towards legalism and an unfor-

giving nature led him to espouse an unbiblical perfectionism
which eventually drove him to heresy.

It is difficult to give a fair assessment of Neander's achievement. Certainly his success in liberating Tertullian from the
confines of Scholasticism was a real gain for scholarship.
Although he was influenced in this by Schleiermacher, he
managed to avoid his master's worst excesses and did much to
remind the academic world that the workings of Divine
Providence could not be reduced to a few logical formulae.
On the other hand, his obsessive opposition to contemporary
rationalism often drove him to conclusions which ill accorded
with a truly scholarly approach. This was particularly true
of his definition of gnosticism. In making Tertullian out to be
its great enemy, Neander was using him as a foil for his own
protest against philosophical trends in nineteenth-century
Germany, a fact which inevitably compromised the book's
value as a contribution to scholarship. On the whole, therefore,
it must be said that *Antignosticus* belongs not so much to the
field of patristic studies as to the world of German romanticism,
from which it drew its chief aims and inspiration.

Neander's subjectivist approach made a great impression
and was not seriously challenged for about a generation.
Eventually, however, there came a renewed attempt to establish a satisfactory objective criterion by which Tertullian's
works could be assessed. Reflecting the secularism which by
then dominated the German universities, the criterion sought
was evolution. In 1848 an unknown student by the name of
Karl Hesselberg[12] submitted an inaugural dissertation to the
University of Dorpat (now Tartu, in Estonia), in which he outlined a scheme of dating which he hoped would arrange
Tertullian's treatises in chronological sequence. Hesselberg
never doubted that Tertullian's intellectual development followed a logical pattern of evolution, and this rather naïve
assumption led him to assign dates to individual treatises on
the basis of the ideas they contained rather than on any hard
evidence. Despite the obvious weakness which this thesis contained, it was taken up by a succession of scholars[13] and
elaborated to absurd lengths. Every scrap of evidence was
culled from the texts in an effort to construct a viable framework for Tertullian's life. The testimony of other ancient

writers was pressed into service, often without sufficient critical examination. The end result of all this research was Ernst Noeldechen's definitive biography, *Tertullian dargestellt*, which appeared in 1890. By that time, however, the chronological objectivist school had largely run out of steam. Its position as the dominant school of thought had been taken over by the neo-romanticism of Adolf Harnack.

Harnack successfully challenged the feasibility of a thorough-going chronological systematisation of Tertullian's works, and pointed scholars back again to the outlook and ideas of Neander.[14] Dissatisfied with the excesses of the dating scheme proposed by Bonwetsch, he replied with a detailed criticism of Hesselberg's original thesis and pointed out the curious mixture of fact and speculation it contained. Harnack of course did not deny the value of chronological study, though occasionally the conclusions he drew were at variance with accepted notions and were certainly far less rigid than those of Hesselberg and his followers. His main objective was to demonstrate that a fixed chronology was not possible in Tertullian's case, and therefore could not offer an objective criterion for interpreting his work. It was useful as a supplementary aid to study, but could never supplant Neander's thesis that it was Tertullian's personality which provided the key to understanding his writings.

But although Harnack followed Neander's main thesis, his work was far from being a carbon-copy of *Antignosticus*. Harnack selected his themes carefully and pursued them to conclusions which Neander would scarcely have recognised. For example, he borrowed the theme of gnosticism which he found in Neander, but unlike him did not restrict the phenomenon to a number of recognised heresies. In Harnack's opinion even the doctrinal statements of the orthodox party represented a rationalistic 'gnostic' corruption of the True Faith. The following passage from *A History of Dogma* (II.2) gives a fair sampling of his attitude:

> How great the innovations actually were, however, may be measured by the fact that they signified a scholastic tutelage of the faith of the individual Christian, and restricted the immediateness of religious feelings and ideas to

the narrowest limits. But the conflict with the so-called Montanism showed that there were still a considerable number of Christians who valued that immediateness and freedom; these were, however, defeated. The fixing of the tradition under the title of apostolic necessarily led to the assumption that whoever held the apostolic doctrine was also essentially a Christian in the apostolic sense. This assumption, quite apart from the innovations which were legitimised by tracing them to the apostles, meant the separation of doctrine and conduct, the preference of the former to the latter, and the transformation of a fellowship of faith, hope and discipline into a communion *eiusdem sacramenti*, that is, into a union which, like the philosophical schools, rested on a doctrinal law, and which was subject to a legal code of divine institution.

From his favourable attitude to the Montanists, it might be thought that Harnack would have followed Neander in portraying Tertullian as the great defender of the true spirit of Christianity. But this was not the case. Harnack did not dispute Tertullian's conversion to Montanism, but he glossed over this rather quickly in order to justify his main thesis which was that Tertullian too was infected by philosophy – in his case, Stoicism – and that it was this, together with his legal training, which determined his approach to Christianity. Fundamentally, therefore, Tertullian had been committed to an alien dogmatism every bit as much as the Greek apologists and the gnostics had been (ibid., p. 79).

Harnack's attacks on Tertullian were accompanied by a rabid anti-Catholicism which was to provoke the ire of Rome[15] and contribute, at least in part, to the unfortunate connection which many Roman Catholics have made between Protestantism and modernism. It is only fair to remember, however, that Harnack's thesis was strongly opposed by competent scholars within the Lutheran Church. His contemporary Siegmund Schlossmann[16] made a detailed study of Tertullian's use of the terms *persona* and *substantia* in the formulation of Trinitarian dogma, and rejected Harnack's thesis that these words were of legal provenance. He claimed instead that ordinary rhetorical usage was sufficient to explain their meaning. Schlossmann was soon followed by H. Koch,[17] who even denied that Tertullian had been a priest, as was generally supposed. Yet although many of Harnack's conclusions were dangerous generalisations, and despite the objections made by fellow scholars, the influence of his thesis has been immense. The combination of a romantic pietism with empirical science caught the mood of the late nineteenth century, with its buoyant, self-confident liberalism. The only opposition, at least in the Protestant world, came from men like Benjamin Warfield,[18] who were clearly swimming against the tide. Everywhere Harnack's views were triumphant – everywhere that is, except in France. The French had preserved a scholarship which could not only rival the German, but which had developed an independent academic tradition only marginally influenced by developments beyond the Rhine.

THE FRENCH ALTERNATIVE

The intellectual forces at work in the eighteenth and nineteenth centuries spread all over Europe, and France felt the impact of the new thought as much as any nation. The reaction there, however, was different from elsewhere, and the consequences for scholarship have made the French tradition unique. The Reformation had left France deeply divided. For a time it had seemed as if the Protestant cause must triumph, but in the end an uneasy truce upheld the Roman establishment, while at the same time granting a considerable measure of toleration to Protestants. Ironically, France thus became the first country in Europe to accept religious pluralism, although the Roman Church never reconciled itself to the fact and regarded the Edict of Nantes as a temporary concession to be withdrawn as soon as it was expedient to do so. The opportunity came in 1685 when Louis XIV, then at the height of his power, decided to crush all possible opposition to his rule. The Protestants were expelled and even the Roman Church was reduced to little more than a department of state. The practical effect of this was to rule out the possibility of a Christian opposition to the monarchy. Grievances henceforth could find an outlet only within a context of secular humanism, a fact which goes far to explain the violently anti-Christian character of the French Revolution.

Throughout the nineteenth century France was plagued by an intermittent civil war with Catholic royalists on one side and atheistic republicans on the other. Battle-lines were firmly drawn, and the compromise which eventually prevailed in Protestant lands was excluded from the start. Faced with open confrontation, the Church had to establish its authority as firmly as possible. Thus it was that with each successive stage of its political collapse, the Roman Church moved one step closer to claiming supreme spiritual authority for itself. The process culminated in 1870, with the fall of Rome following hard on the proclamation of papal infallibility. At the same time, the collapse of the Second Empire in France signalled the victory of the anti-Catholic party, and the long struggle for supremacy entered its final phase. The renewed emphasis on the Pope's spiritual authority was heavily influenced by developments within French Catholicism, and it was in France that the new dogma was most rigorously defended. The keystone in this defence was the claim that the Roman Church alone was authentically apostolic. This claim naturally led to a renewed emphasis on the origins of the Latin Church and this in turn focused attention once more on Tertullian.

The years after 1870 witnessed a spate of theological treatises pouring forth from French seminaries in a concerted effort to establish the perenniality of post-Tridentine Catholic dogma.[19] Although their aims were diametrically opposed to those of their German contemporaries, the strength of mutual indifference was such that no conflict occurred. This phase lasted until about 1890 when the dominance of the ultramontane party began to weaken. German ideas remained only marginally influential, but the liberals of the French Church, tinged as they were with the sociological theories of Auguste Comte and others, had little need of them. In the field of patristic scholarship the new liberalism found its champion in the great historian Paul Monceaux, whose monumental *Histoire littéraire de l'Afrique chrétienne* (1901) has never been surpassed. In this massive work, Monceaux developed the thesis that the North African Church was a sociological entity enjoying a spirituality and culture quite distinct from that of Italy or Gaul. Monceaux began his study, naturally enough, with Tertullian, whom he inclined to regard as the archetype of later Africans. In particular he interpreted Tertullian's flirtation with Montanism as typical of an inherent tendency towards schism which he considered characteristic of African Christianity. Later this tendency gave rise to Donatism, which Monceaux thought was rooted in social and political causes, not theological ones. Monceaux also drew heavily on Tertullian for his portrait of the North African Church as a savagely persecuted body, which compensated for its sufferings with an exaggerated cult of martyrs and martyrdom. His work is invaluable for its breadth and wealth of detail, but it suffers from the limitations of its methodology. In all probability persecution was no more severe in North Africa than elsewhere – certainly Tertullian himself seems never to have suffered from it. Furthermore, its importance in literature has sound theological reasons behind it, and there is no need to posit a North African 'personality' to explain the phenomenon. To prove Monceaux' thesis it would be necessary to demonstrate not only that Africa exhibited a high degree of individuality and uniformity over a long period, but also that this has been accurately reflected in the surviving literature. Unfortunately neither of these things is at all obvious. The writers of the North African Church participated fully in the life of the Oecumene and showed little inclination to develop their separate provincial identity. Their writings are preoccupied with theological matters and other problems are always seen in this light. It is possible that if the whole corpus of Christian literature, and especially of heretical writings, were available to us, we might be able to substantiate Monceaux' claims. But since this is far from being the case at present, his theories must remain highly tentative at best.

In spite of these deficiencies, however, Monceaux' work has exercised a considerable influence on more recent scholarship. Although he professed to be a Catholic, he refused to follow the Church's official teaching and based his research on what were in essence secularist presuppositions. For him, Christianity was not an exclusive system of revealed truth, but a cultural phenomenon which provided an outlet for the religious needs of the people of North Africa from c. AD 150 to c. AD 700.

His English disciple W. H. C. Frend has gone so far as to suggest that there was a fundamental religious continuity between paganism, Christianity and Islam in North Africa. According to him, Christianity failed because it was too closely associated with the power of Rome which the North Africans finally 'rejected' in the eighth century.[20] To this we can only reply that the early Christians were highly conscious that theirs was not a folk-religion, and that they were called to create a new society fundamentally incompatible with the existing culture. It was not pre-existing sociological factors but a consciousness of the living God giving men a burning desire for holiness which decided their outlook. Especially was this true in North Africa, and in the writings of Tertullian in particular. The final triumph of Islam was not coincident with the collapse of Roman power and must be ascribed to other factors, notably the spiritual weakness of the Church long before the Arab conquest and the superficiality of much popular worship, both Donatist and Catholic. Frend's secular viewpoint will not suffice to explain what is in essence a spiritual phenomenon.

Monceaux's liberalism struck at the point where the intellectual armour of Rome was weakest – in its quasi-dualistic conception of 'nature' and 'grace'. Rome, it appeared, could accept a sociological interpretation of the Church as long as it confined itself to the 'natural' realm and left the 'supernatural' side intact. Gaston Boissier, for instance, disapproved of Tertullian's rabid anti-paganism (*La fin du paganisme*, Paris, 1894, Vol. I, p. 270), which he interpreted as a rejection of the good element in 'nature'. According to Boissier, Tertullian fell into heresy because he championed a society built entirely on 'grace'. He saw in him a primitive Jansenist, and contrasted this attitude unfavourably with that of the more liberal Jesuits. Boissier thought Tertullian would have done better had he been willing to adapt pagan customs progressively to Christian needs, instead of rejecting them outright. Boissier claimed to be a good Catholic, but his views scarcely differed from those of Monceaux.

In the years between the appearance of the *Histoire littéraire* and the outbreak of World War I, two important studies of Tertullian appeared. In 1905 came *La théologie de Tertullien* which was modelled on an earlier work by Mgr Freppel. The author, Adhémar d'Alès, stood in the Catholic tradition more firmly than Monceaux, though his work was admirably free of the sort of bias found in Boissier. In his treatment of Tertullian's trinitarian doctrine, for example, d'Alès was careful to point out that post-Nicene categories of thought were inappropriate as guidelines for the earlier period (ibid., p. 103), an admission scarcely calculated to please the more stringent Catholics. He was sceptical too of the real influence of Montanism at Carthage – an interesting point which indicates that he was prepared to question the traditional view that Tertullian had been converted to that heresy (ibid., p. 144).

A few years later the whole question of Tertullian's relationship to Montanism was taken up and examined by Pierre de Labriolle.[21] From the vantage point of Fribourg (Freiburg/ Schweiz) de Labriolle pointed out that Montanism in its Asiatic form had many features which Tertullian would have found repellent. In particular he mentioned the prominence of women in the sect, its lack of discipline and its extreme millenarianism as uncongenial elements. De Labriolle therefore said that it had not been for doctrinal reasons that Tertullian had become a Montanist, but because he had felt a spiritual affinity with the sect's uncompromising demands. De Labriolle provided a link between French and German thought, and was fully conversant with developments in Germany.[22] His methods of research, however, were much more scientific than either Neander's or Harnack's and his conclusions, though less original, are more substantial and deserving of trust.

The only French patristic scholar of the pre-war period who followed the German school more or less faithfully was a professed agnostic, Charles Guignebert.[23] Guignebert's agnosticism is interesting because it shows that Harnack's rabid Protestantism was really superfluous to his argument. Guignebert showed a certain sympathy for Harnack's view that Tertullian's was an authentic evangelical voice of protest against increasing clericalisation, but he did not conclude from this that he ought to become a Protestant. Guignebert undercut Harnack by saying that Protestantism was just as bad as Catholicism, and that only agnosticism could ensure a 'neutral' objectivity. Naturally enough Guignebert's views were attacked on all sides, though subsequent developments have confirmed his approach as the dominant one. Since his time confessional presuppositions have virtually disappeared from scholarly study and a supposedly 'neutral', though in fact secular, methodology has taken their place.

THE AFTERMATH OF LIBERALISM

As is well known, it was the spiritual and intellectual crisis of World War I which broke the back of liberal Protestantism. It was not merely that manuscripts shelved in 1914 seemed out of date four years later; when they emerged again the cultural climate of most of Europe had changed beyond recognition. The unholy alliance of throne and altar, which Karl Barth had so strongly criticised in 1914, collapsed as thrones were toppled and altars deserted by a generation whose attempts to manipulate God had proved so catastrophically futile. Nowhere was the débâcle more evident or more fateful than in Germany, home of liberalism and the Enlightenment. The attempts made by nineteenth-century churchmen to accommodate the 'new thought' to the ancient faith were repudiated when it was realised that what they had done had been to offer religion as a moral adhesive for a state-centred humanism.

The post-war reaction against this type of religion produced a crisis in the theological faculties of Germany. Fundamentally it arose from the age-old problem of reconciling 'nature' and 'grace'. The nineteenth-century liberals had laid heavy stress on the former and were constantly embarrassed by what they regarded as the intrusion of the supernatural into the real world. After the war Karl Barth turned liberalism on its head by stressing 'grace' over 'nature' to the point where the latter almost disappeared from view. Barth's reaction was healthy in that it led theologians back to a more orthodox faith, but his failure to attack and overcome the false distinction between 'nature' and 'grace' meant that his theology never really lost its character as a protest movement. In the end it was unable to counteract the liberalism Barth himself so strongly opposed.

As far as patristic studies were concerned, Barth more or less agreed with Harnack's contention that as time went on the Early Church grew increasingly corrupt. His emphasis was squarely on biblical theology, and under his influence Protestant scholarship turned increasingly away from the Fathers to concentrate exclusively on the Bible. Patristic studies were left, on the whole, to Roman Catholics and those within the Protestant Churches who sympathised with their outlook. Rome had suffered less from liberalism, and the post-war reaction was correspondingly less severe. But even the Roman Church could not impose Tridentine uniformity for ever. The conservatism of the hierarchy concealed both the intellectual barrenness of traditional dogmatics and the new currents of thought which were at work behind the scenes among Catholics dissatisfied with the *status quo*. For a time it seemed that neo-Thomism, which in the early decades of the twentieth century had managed to attract some of the most brilliant minds in France, might counter the drift, but this hope proved to be ephemeral. Like Barthianism, neo-Thomism failed to tackle the problem of the division between 'nature' and 'grace', and in the long term it was used not to oppose but to legitimise the penetration of naturalistic ideas into the Church.

The Roman surrender to secularism can be seen in the development of the *Sondersprache* school in Holland. Under the leadership of Mgr Schrijnen of Nijmegen, this school held that the early Christians used a distinct language of their own to express the mysteries of the Christian faith.

Schrijnen's principal work, *Charakteristik des christlichen Lateins*, appeared in 1932. In it he elaborated his theory that the early Christians were an underground sect which evolved a kind of code language scarcely intelligible to the average pagan Roman. This theory would not have carried much weight had the 'language' been restricted to theological and liturgical terms, which a new religion would bring with it in any case, but Schrijnen and his disciples, among whom Christine Mohrmann is now the leading representative, have pieced together a lengthy vocabulary of *secular* terms, which because they are found only in Christian writers, are assumed to represent the language of this Christian counter-culture.

Schrijnen, however, did not stop here. Within 'Christian Latin' he attempted to distinguish vernacular, ecclesiastical and liturgical varieties, each with its own spirit and sphere of influence. Perhaps the best comment on this attempt has come from L. R. Palmer in *The Latin Language* (London, 1954), p. 195:

It is difficult to see what useful purpose is served by this terminological hair-splitting. Nor need we linger over the problem whether the 'Christianisms' established form merely an 'agglomération' or constitute a system 'sensiblement une'. It is one more of the pseudo-problems created by de Saussure's fatal dichotomy between 'la parole' and 'la langue'.

Palmer writes from a purely linguistic standpoint and does not discuss the theological implications of Schrijnen's theory, but these are very considerable indeed. For in place of a rational religious movement, attacking and conquering the intellectual bastions of pagan society on the strength of verifiable merit, we have a secret sect which sought to overthrow not merely pagan religious beliefs and customs, but even the very structure of logical thought which had prevailed up to then. Furthermore, if Palmer is right in linking Schrijnen's theory to the ideas of de Saussure, then there is clear evidence that the *Sondersprache* school is deeply rooted in a world of romantic humanism, not Christianity. From here it is but a short step to the belief that the human mind, accustomed to 'ordinary' speech, is an inappropriate instrument for comprehending religious truth. We need not wonder that existentialism found such fertile soil in Catholic circles, nor that there should have been such an apparently sudden *rapprochement* between Catholic and secular thinkers.

Naturally Tertullian, as the earliest major Latin Christian writer whose works are largely extant, has occupied a position of particular prominence in the *Sondersprache* scheme. Before Schrijnen scholars had generally assumed that Tertullian's neologisms were either his own invention or else represented borrowings from other disciplines, notably the law, which he adapted to theological use. Harnack, for instance, supposed that Tertullian had lifted words like *persona* and *substantia* from the technical vocabulary of Roman contract law.[24] Schrijnen, however, put forward a theory that these words in Tertullian were no more than *the first recorded instance* of a special Christian vocabulary which had been developing independently of Roman law and classical rhetoric.

Schrijnen's views on Tertullian were elaborated by his colleague Stephan Teeuwen and soon word-studies of various key terms were pouring out.[25] There was even a journal, *Vigiliae Christianae*, which was founded in 1947 partly to propagate the school's ideas. By then, however, the original *Sondersprache* theory was beginning to lose ground. Carl Becker[26] disputed the notion that Tertullian's neologisms were transcriptions of a well-known oral vocabulary, and not long afterwards René Braun[27] was giving the school's assumptions and methods a radical reappraisal. Braun realised that the lack of evidence made it pointless to argue about neologisms or a distinct Christian language. He preferred to compromise by saying that Christians adapted existing words to specialised religious uses. Fundamentally, however, although he did not follow the advocates of *Sondersprache* all the way, he agreed with them that the best approach to Tertullian's work lay in a minute analysis of his vocabulary. His own work attracted a number of disciples, mostly in France, and these perpetuate the tradition of linguistic analysis.

Lexical study now plays such an important role in any research on Tertullian that it is difficult to examine it critically or propose an acceptable alternative. Yet the approach contains such obvious weaknesses that some attempt must be made to do this. The *Sondersprache* school and its descendants assumed too readily that individual words possess fixed meanings which make studying them in isolation profitable for elucidating the development of a theological system. In fact, of course, linguistic precision was just what did *not* exist much before Nicaea, and it was this lack which contributed so much to the dogmatic debates of the third and fourth centuries. The difficulty which Tertullian experienced in trying to find a suitable Latin translation for the Greek *logos* – surely a key concept – is sufficient reminder that the 'Church language' posited by Schrijnen has little basis in fact.[28]

It is a pity that patristic scholarship has not yet found a James Barr to perform the work of demolition these lexical theories so urgently need. It is simply not true to say that the early Christians used a separate language in theology and worship. Their Latin was the common speech of all Romans and followed the same general evolution. The many Graecisms and neologisms which occur in their writings are typical of the period, as a perusal of Juvenal or Martial will testify. To some extent the needs of popular propaganda emancipated them from the norms of classical style, but this was only to bring them closer to popular speech and did not produce an esoteric vocabulary. Naturally, since Christianity was a new and distinctive religion with a Semitic, rather than a Graeco-Roman background, Christian writers found themselves introducing new words and speech-patterns into Latin. Some established words took on new shades of meaning as they were adapted to Christian theology. But it cannot be stressed too strongly that this adaptation almost invariably followed the native genius of the language and did no more than exploit possibilities and tendencies latent within it. The Fathers always sought the most appropriate existing words in which to express their thoughts, and coined new ones only when this was necessary. It is no exaggeration to say that their entire mental outlook on this matter was diametrically opposed to any theory of a *Sondersprache.*

It is in their ideas, not in their vocabulary, that the mind of the Latin Fathers is to be sought. A fundamental principle of the Incarnation is that the Divine has been expressed in terms which men can understand, without either compromising the transcendence of the former or belittling the autonomy of the latter. In other words, the truth about God may be accurately expressed in human words and thought-patterns, although these can never contain or limit the nature of God. This point is important because it is here that modern theologians of the 'radical' kind differ most profoundly from their ancient counterparts. Unless the implications of the Incarnation for the intellect are understood, it is impossible to comprehend a man like Tertullian. The linguistic analysis of his works is pointless in itself, since unlike modern scholars, Tertullian did not have a superstitious reverence for his vocabulary. Nor was he interested in writing in a language which only the initiated could understand. His aim was always to express in the common tongue the great truths of the Gospel, so that the whole of Roman life and thought might be brought into subjection to Christ. In this sense it may truly be said that his work had one underlying purpose – to conform the tangible pagan world to the principles of Christ. Any theory, therefore, which proposes the existence of a separate religious language must be rejected, in that it is incompatible with Tertullian's basic aims. Had such a language existed, Christianity would have been little different from one of the mystery religions, and in the long term it probably would have suffered the same fate as they did.

THE CURRENT SCENE

The dominance which the *Sondersprache* school has maintained until quite recently is symptomatic of the current state of Tertullian studies. Even those who have criticised its lexical approach have been deeply influenced by it, and the general taste for technicalities continues unabated. Timothy Barnes expressed it well when he said of Tertullian that '... for the most part, the task of setting him in his historical context or cultural milieu has been shirked. Scholarly attention has been happily engrossed on peripheral problems or isolated aspects of Tertullian's thought and writings'.[29]

With a clarity of purpose which is admirable in any scholar, Barnes set out to remedy this defect in an extensive study of his own, which touches on every aspect of Tertullian's life. Barnes has brought together many of the isolated studies which he mentions, and in this book attempts to put them in perspective. He is fully aware that lack of evidence makes it impossible to write a biography of the man in the usual sense, and he has made no attempt to do this. Instead, he has sketched for us the main factors at work in Tertullian's spiritual and cultural formation, including such important things as persecution, martydom and the syllabus of a pagan schoolboy's education. Inevitably, this approach takes us beyond what we can glean from Tertullian's writings alone, and the composite picture which Barnes has drawn is a possible reconstruction rather than a documented history.

In itself, this is not necessarily a bad thing, and much of what Barnes has to say offers a valuable corrective to the popular notion that Tertullian was a lawyer-priest who left the

Church just as he was about to be excommunicated for heresy. Some of his hypotheses are questionable, like his assertion that the unknown bishop attacked in *De pudicitia* was a bishop of Carthage, and others are purely guesswork, as when he suggests that Tertullian was born about AD 170 (when most scholars prefer a date *c.* AD 155), but these are minor idiosyncracies on points where no real knowledge is possible.

A more serious criticism of Barnes' approach is that by centring interest on Tertullian's intellectual and cultural background he has executed a portrait of the man which is out of focus. Like it or not, we know almost nothing of Tertullian beyond the texts which he has left us, and the living power of his mind can only be sought in them, not around them. Barnes has used Tertullian's writings as a quarry from which to extract material suitable for building a framework of his own design; he has not illuminated the inner structure of Tertullian's own thought. The result is that the texts have been plundered in what (to an outside observer) is a haphazard fashion.

The simple fact is that Tertullian's writings cannot be understood from a study of his background and circumstances alone. It is no accident that the modern scholar finds it difficult to extract reliable information of this kind from the texts; Tertullian himself would not have wished it otherwise. Conscious as he was of the impermanence of this world's glory, it was never his desire to speak of his own record and achievements. For him the only thing which mattered in life was to know God in the person of his Son Jesus Christ, and as St Paul says in Philippians 3.9, to be found in him, not having his own righteousness, but that which is through faith in Christ. The student who would understand Tertullian must understand above all that his life was the pursuit of holiness in the presence of the living God. It is this crying need which his writings seek to impress on their readers, and which gives to his genius a universality which none of his contemporaries, despite their similar background and experiences, managed to achieve. It is therefore as we study his struggle for sanctification that our mind reaches out to one who has walked before us in the early pilgrimage of faith and gives us a deeper awareness of his true stature as a writer and a Christian.

CHAPTER TWO

THE MAN AND HIS TIMES

THE PAGAN BACKGROUND

Quintus Florens Septimius Tertullianus, the man we call Tertullian, was born at Carthage (near the modern Tunis) sometime in the third quarter of the second century AD. The city had had a long and distinguished history of nearly a thousand years at the time of his birth, and every Roman schoolboy knew by heart the epic struggle which Rome had waged with Carthage for control of the Western Mediterranean. The first foundation of the city under the beautiful queen Dido, herself a refugee from distant Phoenicia, had long been wrapped in legend and immortalised by the genius of Virgil. In historical times Carthage had once been mistress of the seas, and her traders, like those of metropolitan Tyre, had explored the limits of the known world. In the second century BC, Punic, the Carthaginian language (closely related to Hebrew and Arabic), was widely understood at Rome, as we know from the comic poet Plautus, who felt able to use it in the dialogue of one of his plays.[1] By then, however, the great days were already over, and Rome was in the ascendant.

For over a century there was intermittent warfare between the two cities, and the great Carthaginian Hannibal very nearly captured Rome after destroying the legions at Cannae (216 BC). In the event he missed his opportunity and Rome dramatically recovered. The theatre of war shifted to Africa, where at the great battle of Zama (202 BC) the military might of Carthage was shattered for ever. The city survived, in greatly reduced circumstances, until its final destruction at the end of the Third Punic War (149–146 BC). The memory of Rome's peril lingered on, however, and Cato the Elder's famous words, *Carthago delenda est* ('Carthage must be destroyed'), etched themselves deep in the national consciousness. For a century the site lay desolate, to be refounded by Julius Caesar as a

Roman colony (46 BC). As such Carthage became a centre of the purest Latinity, and gradually extended its cultural sway to the still largely Semitic interior.

By Tertullian's time, the wealth and prosperity of Carthage had made it the second city of the West. Its schools were famous all over the Empire, and its trade was perhaps even more important than it had been in Phoenician times. The irrigation of the fertile plains up-country had given the city a prosperous base which it was not to lose until the devastations of civil strife in AD 238. Even then its importance hardly diminished and some of the greatest names in late antiquity lived and worked there. In the second century these included the great novelist Apuleius, whose satirical comedies give a brilliant picture of high society in Tertullian's youth. It was a carefree, enlightened age, though not without a darker side, as Tertullian and his fellow Christians discovered to their cost.

Tertullian's family background is obscure, and all attempts to enlighten us on it have proved unsatisfactory. We know that he was born into a well-to-do pagan household, but we do not know the source of its prosperity. According to Jerome, Tertullian's father had been a centurion in the imperial army. This may contain an element of truth, but as Jerome calls him a *centurio proconsularis*, rank which to our knowledge did not exist in the Roman army, his statement must be treated with some caution.[2]

Tertullian's writings indicate that he had received a sound training in philosophy, classical literature and the law, though there is little sign that he was particularly erudite in any of these disciplines. Eusebius (*Hist. eccl.* ii.2.4) claimed that he was a brilliant jurist, but this cannot be proved. Many people have identified him with an obscure lawyer called Tertullianus, who apparently lived about the same time, but this is now thought to be improbable. His legal training was doubtless sufficient to impress a Greek historian with little knowledge of the subject, but there are curious gaps which do not convince modern scholars. In particular, his understanding of the legal basis for the persecution of Christians is sketchy at best, and is nowadays generally thought to be wrong (see below).

The nature and extent of Tertullian's legal education has been a matter for controversy ever since Schlossmann denied

Harnack's assertion that it was his professional juristic training which led Tertullian to define the doctrine of the Trinity in legal terms. Supporting Harnack were James Morgan and Alexander Beck, who undertook a lengthy refutation of Harnack's critics.[3] Beck's views, however, have not convinced more recent scholars, and the general weight of opinion now favours Schlossmann. This is substantially the position held by Sider, Fredouille and Barnes, although there are still some scholars who tend more towards Harnack's view.[4] On balance there seems little doubt that Schlossmann was right to insist that Tertullian was not a professional lawyer, although his formal education certainly gave him substantial legal knowledge. Tertullian frequently used legal terminology and cast his arguments in a forensic mould, but there is little sign of the detailed knowledge one would expect from a professional jurist.[5]

On the broader question Tertullian's familiarity with classical literature, no comprehensive study of the evidence has as yet been attempted. Given the scantiness of the sources and the limitations of the work which has been done, perhaps this is just as well. Shortly before the last war, Adhémar d'Alès wrote an article outlining Tertullian's knowledge of the Greek poets, and Braun has found traces of Virgil, Lucretius and Juvenal in his works.[6] The difficulty, of course, is that Tertullian seldom mentions classical writers by name, so that there is a good deal of speculation involved in assigning the alleged 'quotations'. Furthermore, investigations of this sort are inevitably superficial and usually miss the point. This is the case with Timothy Barnes, for instance, who has maintained that because Tertullian was familiar with Tacitus and Juvenal, we may consider him to have been more erudite than Jerome.[7] Barnes, of course, has ignored the influence of the third-century Ciceronian revival which led to the virtual eclipse of Silver Age writing in the late Empire. Jerome did not quote Tacitus at least partly because at that time he was an unfashionable and little-read author. At a more serious level, however, Barnes' statement begs the question as to whether it is breadth or depth of learning which is the true hallmark of erudition. Not casual allusions but substance is what really counts in estimating the extent of Tertullian's classicism. When viewed in this light, it may be said that research into Tertullian's literary background has scarcely begun.

More extensive than the search for literary allusions, if not necessarily more fruitful, have been the attempts to connect him with various strands of ancient philosophy. Neander raised the problem, but 'solved' it by saying that Tertullian was basically an antiphilosophical writer. A more positive note was struck by Gerhard Esser[8] who traced Tertullian's teaching on the soul to the influence of Stoicism, a view which was to gain wide support later on. After Harnack there appeared a definite shift in scholarly opinion which was reflected in the work of Schelowsky,[9] who maintained that Tertullian was unwittingly seduced by the philosophical ideas he was trying to combat, so that in the end he became a supporter of the philosophical speculation he so vehemently opposed. Schelowsky also claimed, in opposition to the orthodox Protestant views put forward by Hauschild,[10] that Tertullian accepted 'nature' as a source of Divine Revelation equal to Scripture. This idea was later seized upon by the Catholic Fuetscher[11] who also rejected Hauschild's views.

Fuetscher's work, in the best Thomist tradition, simply assumed that Tertullian employed philosophy as the hand-maid of theology. This attitude has prevailed in Catholic circles to this day, and the main question has been which philosophy it was that Tertullian was most attached to. Various attempts have been made to find allusions to Aristotle in his writings but these have not been particularly convincing[12] and the general opinion now favours Stoicism as the main impetus behind Tertullian's philosophical speculations. This view was most forcefully set out by Jan Waszink in his monumental edition of the De anima. But although Waszink may fairly be said to represent the mainstream in modern research, his view does not completely dominate the field. André Festugière, for example, has maintained that Tertullian lacked a coherent philosophical system, and that in so far as he indulged in philo-sophical speculation at all, it was based on a nebulous frame-work of 'platonic gnosticism'.[13] Following the Stoic line, how-ever, have been Heinrich Karpp and Michel Spanneut[14] who have both traced Tertullian's views to the influence of Soranus. On the other hand, Lazzati's attempt to demonstrate his dependence on Cicero has been effectively discounted by Ilona Opelt[15] and future research in this area is unlikely to produce more positive results.

The debate over the philosophers, however, is only one side of the picture. At the same time that all this has been going on, a vigorous tradition has grown up asserting that Tertullian was basically an antiphilosophical writer. J. Lebreton,[16] for instance, thought that Tertullian's uncompromising stand was to be explained by his desire to attack the 'evil' of Christian speculation. G. J. de Vries[17] has denied that Tertullian was in any sense a philosopher and has insisted that his famous *credo quia absurdum*[18] be taken literally. In this he was followed by Gustave Bardy,[19] though not by André Labhardt, who claimed that the *absurdum* referred not to Tertullian's disquiet at pagan rationalism, but to the 'foolish things of God' he mentions in the preceding lines.[20] Labhardt nevertheless maintained that Tertullian was opposed to philosophy on principle, and not just because the philosophies he knew were of pagan origin. The Jesuit scholar R. F. Refoulé[21] has since attempted to modify Labhardt's *position pure* by saying that Tertullian put great stress on baptism as the means for removing the barrier of man's understanding. It may be doubted, however, whether Refoulé will have much influence on this school of thought, since his concept of sin as mere deprivation, without necessarily including an element of guilt and responsibility, is unsatisfactory.

In view of the conflicting opinions regarding Tertullian's attitude to philosophy, can any positive conclusions be drawn? One of the fairest judgments is that of Claude Tresmontant, who states that Tertullian habitually adopted his opponent's standpoint and proceeded from there to demonstrate its inconsistencies. According to Tresmontant, he neither had a philosophical system nor chose one eclectically from among the many available. When compared with biblical teaching, his writings betray the lingering influence of pagan thought-patterns, especially on the subject of the relationship between the body and the soul. In Tresmontant's own words:

Tertullian, like all the Fathers, understands by 'the flesh' a substance distinct from 'the soul', which is contrary to

Biblical usage. By defending 'the flesh' against its Gnostic detractors, Tertullian recovers a necessity which is in effect genuinely inherent in Christian anthropology, which is based on Biblical anthropology. But, like most of the Fathers, Tertullian is the prisoner of an anthropological dualism at the same time as he is attacking this very thing, in the name of the metaphysical principles of Christianity. Like most of the Fathers, Tertullian takes the resurrection of the flesh, or the body, to be the resurrection of *something other than the soul.* There are thus *two* things, *two* substances, connected yet distinct from each other, which, according to Tertullian, must rise again.[22]

In focussing his attention on the relationship between the body and the soul, Tresmontant has gone beyond the superficial question of sources and hit upon one of the central problems of his whole outlook. It is not a problem which can be traced with certainty to a particular philosophical school; rather it is a more general phenomenon which exerted a powerful influence over all branches of ancient thought.

Tertullian's political views have also come under scrutiny in recent years. The traditional opinion has always been that Tertullian advocated total separation from the world and all its works, and this view has not been completely abandoned.[23] But recent studies have shown a marked tendency to reverse the separatist position common a generation ago, and Tertullian has now been made to appear as the great defender of the Empire, who insisted only that Christians be treated fairly within it.[24] No doubt the more recent picture reflects growing concern for social and political involvement in the modern Church, though it is probably true to say that even when allowance is made for this, the new emphasis does greater justice to Tertullian's source of practicality and his awareness of the importance of the material world in God's plan of salvation, than older theories which concentrated too exclusively on his exhortations to follow the example of the martyrs.

From the foregoing it will be apparent that there is much to be said about Tertullian's social and cultural background, even in spite of our lack of specific information. On the other hand, it is equally clear that it must all be seen in the light of his subsequent Christian commitment, without which it would have little coherence or meaning. Tertullian's conversion was without a doubt the single most important event in his life, as indeed it is in the life of any Christian, though here again we can say virtually nothing about it. Like so many others, he surrendered to Christ in early manhood, but we cannot date this with any confidence, except that it must have been sometime before AD 197. The usual conjecture is that he was converted about AD 193, the year in which Septimius Severus laid claim to the Empire; but this is only a guess. The most important occurrence in Tertullian's life is shrouded in darkness and, as with so much else, can be known only from its effects in later years.

THE SECOND-CENTURY CHURCH

Our first glimpse of Tertullian the Christian finds him securely within the fold of the Church at Carthage. Whether his contact with this congregation antedated his conversion to any significant degree is of course impossible to say, and we know hardly anything about the depth or nature of his commitment to the assembly of believers in its institutional form. On the other hand, we do know, both from his own testimony and from that of his contemporaries, a good deal of what the Church of his time was like, and what it expected of its members.

Beginning as a breakaway sect from Judaism about AD 30 (the date most usually agreed for the death, resurrection and ascension of Jesus, followed by the descent of the Holy Spirit at Pentecost), the Christian Church quickly spread across the Mediterranean world. Within fifty years congregations of believers had been established in all the main cities and towns of the East, as well as at Rome. An originally Jewish leadership was giving way to Greek, and the new religion soon gained a firm foothold wherever traders and other travellers congregated. In contrast with its competitors, Christianity claimed no land as its home, no antiquity as its pedigree. Christians of every race and tongue were a new nation, called out from the world and set aside as the heralds and first-fruits of the coming Kingdom of God.

When Christianity first came to North Africa is impossible

to say. A great city like Carthage can hardly have been without a church for very long, but its earliest history is unknown. Analogy with two other Western cities, Rome and Lyons, suggests that the first congregation was Greek-speaking and thus consisted mainly of transients and expatriates. More controversial is the suggestion that this Greek element was largely Jewish. This thesis has been strongly defended in recent years by the late Cardinal Jean Daniélou[25] but his hypotheses remain unconvincing. It is certainly true that Tertullian frequently attacked Judaism and the Jews, but it remains doubtful to what extent he was referring to contemporaries, jealous of the success of the Christians, as opposed to the Jews of the Bible. Until this question can be resolved in Daniélou's favour, the theory that North African Christianity sprang directly from Jewish roots must be regarded as unproved, at least from Tertullian's writings.

What we do know, however, is that Carthage was the cradle of Latin Christianity, for it was here that the Church first abandoned Greek and adopted the local language in its worship and instruction. Indigenisation was undoubtedly a gradual process and may not have been fully completed when Tertullian began his career, since he wrote at least some of his works in Greek as well as in Latin. Nevertheless, by AD 190 the Carthaginian church was ready and eager to receive Christian teaching in the native tongue. Whatever dissensions this literature might later provoke, it was at least certain that Tertullian's genius would not be sweetness wasted on the desert air.

The inner life of this church, its worship and organisation, is not known to us in detail. About all we know for sure is that regular meetings were held, at which prayer was offered to God, hymns were sung, and the Word was preached, perhaps by someone who was charismatically gifted. We do not know whether every service centred around the eucharist; this is frequently assumed, but it cannot be proved. It is somewhat remarkable, for instance, that although Tertullian seems to tell us a great deal about the life and piety of ordinary Christians (if only to criticise them) he says almost nothing about the communion service. Clearly the order of priorities, or at least the focus of interest, at Carthage was not eucharistic, as it was to become later on. In Tertullian's day the Lord's supper was an act of worship within the community, but it did not attract the same interest as baptism, or the many expressions of personal piety on which he attempts to legislate.

The ministry of the Church is equally obscure. The New Testament records three names given to Church officers – bishop (*episkopos*), elder (*presbyteros*) and deacon (*diakonos*). Real authority, however, resided in the apostles (*apostoloi*), who exercised an itinerant ministry and did not hesitate to advise congregations from a distance. By the end of the first century the apostles were all dead, and they were not replaced. Instead the three orders mentioned above were left to divide the work of the ministry among them.

How was this done? Most scholars today agree that the duties and functions of a bishop are reasonably clear. He governed the church as the Apostle's representative, and was responsible for ensuring that their teaching was maintained in its fullness and in its purity. It is uncertain whether bishops were appointed to a congregation or to a place, though in the first two centuries this would not have mattered, since there was seldom more than one congregation in any one locality. The role of the deacon is likewise fairly clear: he was charged with pastoral and administrative duties so that the bishop could be free to preach the Gospel.

But what are we to make of the elder? It seems entirely possible, as even Jerome believed,[26] that initially at least, bishops and elders were one and the same. The author of 2 and 3 John would seem to come into this category, since he describes himself as an elder yet advises the Church like a bishop. If he was the Apostle John, then such a conclusion necessarily imposes itself. At the same time, however, there was never more than one bishop in a congregation (as far as we know), but elders were numerous. It seems likely, therefore, that from a very early stage, the bishop was at least first among equals. As the chief presbyter, the conduct of worship, especially the celebration of the eucharist, would normally be his responsibility, though in his absence another presbyter would stand in his stead.

As the Church grew in size, delegation of episcopal responsibilities to the presbyters became common, and they were eventually assigned congregations and parishes of their own. What we do not know, however, is how far this process had advanced by Tertullian's time. The matter is of some importance, since Jerome claimed that Tertullian was an elder (*presbyter*) at Carthage. Now Tertullian cannot have been a bishop, so the system of Church government must have evolved somewhat from what Jerome supposed had been its most primitive stage. Some scholars have maintained that Jerome was merely guessing at Tertullian's status, on the assumption that such a distinguished person would never have been a layman. These scholars point out that there is no evidence that Tertullian ever exercised the functions of a presbyter – particularly in respect of the eucharist.

This, however, depends entirely on what we understand those functions to have been at that time. Unfortunately the whole issue has been complicated by subsequent developments in eucharistic theology, which introduced an element of sacrifice into the celebrant's action. Parallels were drawn with the Old Testament sacrifices, and before long the words *presbyter* and *sacerdos* (used of a man who offered a sacrifice) became confused. The result is that modern languages, including English, have only the one word *priest* (derived from *presbyter*) to cover both meanings. Thus it has been argued that Tertullian cannot have been a *presbyter* because he was not, so it seems, a priest in the sacerdotal sense. Yet it is quite possible that he was an elder as outlined above, in the days before eucharistic sacrifice became an accepted doctrine. Far from being wrong, Jerome may have preserved the memory of an earlier time, in which a Calvinist would have been more at home than a modern Catholic.

What is certain is that worship and liturgy were not aspects of church life which greatly preoccupied Tertullian. His own interests were determined much more by the pressures which Christianity was facing from without. These were of two kinds. The first and more blatant was physical persecution, the danger of which exercised a powerful formative influence on the young Church's mind. The second, and more subtle, was the intellectual challenge of pagan philosophies and religions, which in the second century threatened to overwhelm the nascent theology of the Christians. It was against this background of a double threat to the Church's very existence that

Tertullian was forced to work out his own understanding of the Faith.

THE NOBLE ARMY OF MARTYRS

There is probably no aspect of the Early Church which has been more widely discussed, or celebrated over as long a period, as the phenomenon of martyrdom. Almost from the very beginning persecution was a fact of life in the early community, and this could not fail to create a deep and lasting impression. Our sources generally agree that in the earliest period the greatest danger came from the Jews. This was inevitable, not only because the first Christians were almost all converts from Judaism, but also because they taught a faith which profoundly scandalised Jewish theological opinion, in whose eyes it was deeply subversive. St Paul concentrated his initial evangelistic efforts on Jewish communities in the Diaspora, where more often than not his teaching aroused the ire of the elders, who were not above appealing for redress to the Roman magistrate (Acts 17.6; 18.12, etc.).

The fact that it was the Jews who had the most to lose from the spread of the new faith explains both the depth and the persistence of their hostility towards it. The Roman reaction to their agitation was initially restrained, as the New Testament evidence indicates. Tertullian even thought that Tiberius had shown favour to the Christians (*Apol.* 5.2), and this is by no means impossible. It would have been a perfectly natural reaction for a pagan ruler, on hearing of a new religion, to tolerate it in the expectation that it would soon be integrated into a wider syncretistic whole. Again, there is evidence from the New Testament to indicate that some pagans at least may have welcomed the new faith with precisely these intentions (Acts 14.11–18).

It was not until the reign of Nero that the Roman authorities began to persecute Christians as a separate sect. Tacitus (*Ann.* 15.44) tells us that this was because Nero needed a scapegoat on which to lay the blame for the great fire of Rome in AD 64. Tertullian refers to this *institutum Neronianum* (*Ad nat.* i.7.9; *Apol.* 5.3 ff.) and claims that it was the basis of the legalised persecutions in later times. This has been hotly contested by modern scholars, and the vagueness of the word *institutum* is not much help, but even if Nero's order had no permanent legal effect, it undoubtedly did set a precedent for persecution which no subsequent emperor, until Constantine, repudiated. For two centuries public denunciation (*delatio*) continued to provoke the execution of convinced Christians.

But who denounced them, and why? Tertullian tells us that in his day Christians had become the universal bogeymen, prime targets for mob violence (*Apol.* 40.1–2). The impression he gives is that this violence was quite irrational and had no basis whatever in fact. If this is true, then who incited the mobs? W. H. C. Frend has consistently argued that the chief culprits were the Jews.[27] In a series of articles he has argued that Tertullian's statement about the Jewish synagogues as founts of persecution (*Scorp.* 10.10) is not to be understood merely in a historical sense, but also as a living reality. When we consider that in addition to the reasons mentioned above, the Jews at this time were concerned to deflect prejudice away from themselves, this is quite possible. On the other hand, it does not accord well with the famous description of the mob in *Apologeticum*, where there is no mention of Jews. Probably they were responsible for some of the agitation, but in times of crisis pagan nerves must have flared up easily, and the Christians, once under suspicion, would have remained favourite scapegoats.

From the purely historical point of view, Tertullian's accounts of martyrdom are surprisingly weak, and rely on anachronism more than Frend might allow. Despite his approval of martyrdom, for instance, Tertullian says virtually nothing about the actual martyrs themselves. The only ones he mentions by name are Perpetua, Justin and Rutilius, and even then it is only in passing.[28] This is all the more surprising when we remember that Perpetua was his contemporary, and that he may conceivably have witnessed her death.[29] How can this lack of detail be explained, if martyrdom was of such obvious importance?

The main reason seems to be that Tertullian lived in a period of relative calm in which very few Christians were put to death.[30] The African Church in particular, although it was later to become famous for its martyrs, suffered very little persecution before the death of Septimius Severus in AD 211. It so happens that we have two accounts of incidents in which Christians were put to death, but these tend to confirm rather than dispel this impression. The first is the well-known *Acts of the Scillitan Martyrs*, according to which a number of villagers were sentenced to death at Carthage in AD 180. Tertullian does not mention this incident at all, though he almost certainly knew of it. It is hard to see why this should be so, except that for some reason he did not think it important enough. The account of the Scillitans dovetails remarkably well with the famous letter of Pliny the Younger to Trajan (*Ep.* 10.97), in which he describes to the emperor how he handled this sort of thing in Bithynia during his governorship there (AD 112–13). Pliny's account seems to imply that cases of this kind were fairly routine, and the martyrs at Scilli may be exceptional only in that an account of their ordeal has been preserved. In the case of Perpetua and Felicity, martyred in AD 203, there is strong evidence that they were somehow connected with Tertullian, and it has even been conjectured, though somewhat less than convincingly, that he was the author of the account of their martyrdom.[31]

The striking fact about all this, however, is that nobody of any standing in the Church was affected – in marked contrast to the situation a generation earlier, when both Justin and Polycarp had suffered death from persecution. The conclusion that Tertullian's concentration on martyrdom as a phenomenon was out of all proportion to the reality, at least as it was experienced by him, seems inescapable. But, fortunately, there is a ready explanation for this apparently curious phenomenon. By the late second century martyrdom was already a stock theme of Christian literature, and hagiography was starting to appear as a genre in its own right. It seems that there were already the beginnings of a cult of Polycarp at Smyrna, although the main developments along this line were still in the future.[32] The chief elements of this literature were simple enough. The example of Christ and the Apostles, and the rewards of the heavenly kingdom, were stressed as incentives to persevere against all odds.[33] Faithfulness to the end was the hallmark of the true Christian.[34] Moreover, it was the only sure guarantee of salvation, since the blood of martyrs was sufficient to wipe away sin.[35] Some, like Clement of Alexandria, took a milder view of the whole question, but they were exceptional.[36] Tertullian threw himself into the mainstream with gusto, and even hinted that heaven was a place reserved *exclusively* for martyrs.

But although Tertullian certainly borrowed his main theme from Eastern sources, his attitude towards martyrdom reflects concerns which were peculiarly his own. This may be seen from *Ad martyras*. This work says virtually nothing about following the example set by Christ, although there are references to his teaching. Heavenly rewards are hardly mentioned. The 'martyrs' whom he celebrates are not even Christians – a highly revealing fact. All of them without exception are figures drawn from pagan history and mythology. Obviously, fidelity to Christ was not the most important element in Tertullian's definition of a martyr!

Indeed, of all the aspects of martyrdom which the Early Church celebrated, it was the notion that the victims should display a worthiness (*dignitas*) to meet their fate which most impressed Tertullian. As far as he was concerned, the greatest danger to a prospective martyr was that he would succumb, not so much to the fear of death, as to the temptations of the world. He therefore concentrated his attention on the martyrs' need for stringent spiritual exercises in prison in order that they might subdue the flesh in advance. If martyrdom could be compared to a battle, then spiritual discipline was the necessary training for success at the moment of crisis. And whereas no one could know when he might be called to sacrifice his life, everyone could prepare himself against the eventuality by a life of strict and consistent discipline.

The most striking thing about *Ad martyras* is not what it says about martyrdom, which is rather little, but what it recalls in the ascetic literature of the East. For instance, we are told that prison in the life of a Christian was the equivalent of the desert for the prophets of old. Immediately our thoughts turn to the subsequent history of eremitic spirituality, with its strong ascetic emphasis. Likewise the military imagery associated with spiritual warfare, though indisputably Roman in tone, reminds us of the 'holy war' which the Syrian Fathers found so important.[37]

Was Tertullian then influenced by a primitive form of this

asceticism? Great caution is required here. On the one hand, we know that he was well acquainted with Eastern heresies like Marcionism and Valentinianism, and many of his reactions to their proposals bear an astonishing similarity to what was taught by the orthodox party among the Syrians, at least at a later date. On the other hand, there is no hint in Tertullian's extant works that he had any positive dealings with them. The comparison between prison and the desert was quite possibly his own invention; in any case he says only that the Old Testament prophets went there, and does not mention contemporary Christians. The language of spiritual warfare could easily have been derived from St Paul (cf. Eph. 6.10–19; 2 Tim. 4.7) and need not be of Syrian provenance. If Robert Murray is right in thinking that the early Syrians derived their idea of the 'holy war' from Qumran, where the ascetic interest far outweighed the martyrological, then it is unlikely that Tertullian (for whom martyrdom was the stated goal of the ascetic life), got his ideas from them.

Ad martyras provides us with an interesting example of how martydom, in theory the focus of interest, gave way in practice to a more immediate emphasis on asceticism. This impression is confirmed by *De fuga in persecutione* where Tertullian gives a detailed explanation of the cosmic forces at work behind the phenomenon of persecution. Asked to decide whether persecution came from God or from the devil, he replied with a detailed argument in which he maintained that ultimately it came from God, who used the devil as his instrument. But how could such an evil thing be in the mind of God? The answer was that persecution was not really an evil but a test of faith. For those who walked in the Spirit there was nothing to fear; rather they rejoiced that the judgment of God had vindicated their faith (*De fuga* 4).

The concept of persecution as a judgment is brought out more specifically in *Scorpiace*. In this treatise Tertullian claims that persecution had arisen as a punishment for heresy and idolatry. It may be compared with the plague of serpents brought on by Israel's apostasy in the desert (*Scorp.* 2–3). *Scorpiace* is less polished than *De fuga*, and Tertullian shows himself to be less inclined to reasoned argument. There is none of the latter's detailed apologetic; instead *Scorpiace* consists almost entirely of

lengthy quotations from Scripture, interspersed with an appropriate commentary to reinforce the message.

Thus we find in Tertullian's works on martyrdom, a shift
away from the punishment itself and a new emphasis on the
ascetic life of preparation. The concept of martyrdom as a
judgment is emphasised, and the saving power of martyrdom
alone played down. Tertullian never denied that a martyr was
certain of his heavenly reward, but that was not the main
focus of his attention. After all, what was there to distinguish
a martyr from any ordinary person who was put to death?
Augustine was later to remark that it was the cause, not the
punishment, which validated a man's claim to martyrdom (cf.
Epp. 61; 167: *martyros veros non facit poena, sed causa*), implying
that it was the Christian's glory to suffer for the precious Name
of Christ. But although Tertullian would hardly have disagreed
with such a statement, his own emphasis was more subjective.
For him the distinguishing mark of a martyr was the victim's
worthiness to face the supreme challenge. For that reason, a
man who expected to crown his earthly life with the blood of
martyrdom must make sanctification his chief pursuit in the
interval.

THE WAY OF FAITH

The idea that persecution was a punishment inflicted on the
Church as a scourge for its failure to wipe out heresy will not
seem strange to anyone acquainted with early Christian
apocalyptic literature. Its importance as a theme in Tertullian's
writings should not be underestimated, since it gives us a good
idea of the weight which he attached to right belief in the life
of the Church. It scarcely matters if the word orthodoxy itself
is an anachronism here, since the existence of a standard of
correct doctrine is clearly assumed in his writings. Quite apart
from the numerous and length refutations of different heresies,
which in bulk comprise more than a third of the extant
corpus, there is Tertullian's steady insistence that Christian faith
and discipline must be governed by an authoritative rule
(*regula*). Whether this means that there was a formal Rule of
Faith (*regula fidei*) to which Christians were expected to sub-
scribe is a matter of dispute, and must be considered uncertain,

but it is beyond question that Tertullian appealed to an objective standard of belief of some sort, which he claimed as normative for the Church.

This standard may well have varied somewhat in its formulation, if it can be said to have been consciously formulated at all, but the general outline of its contents is fairly clear. In essence it consisted of a profession of belief in the Triune God, with a particular emphasis on the Person and Work of the Son, Jesus Christ. In this connection it is a matter of some interest that Tertullian gives a résumé of the faith in forms which are remarkably similar to the so-called Apostles' Creed, a later confession which was probably modelled to some extent on them. This similarity, and especially the claim made by later generations that even the very form of words in the creed could be traced back to the Apostles, is of more than merely passing interest, for it reminds us of a fundamental conviction, which all the orthodox party shared, that the propositions of the creed represented the authentic teaching of the Apostles, and that this teaching had been handed on in the Church in an unbroken line of succession. This belief constituted the main line of defence against the heretics, who were accused of teaching novelties which departed from the true faith (cf., e.g. *De praescr. haer.* 29).

But was Tertullian right to believe this? The traditional view that heresy is an aberrant novelty *vis-à-vis* an orthodoxy of apostolic origin has been seriously challenged in modern times and today it is probably true to say that most scholars, even the more conservative, believe that the polarisation between orthodoxy and heresy was a late second-century development in what had previously been a broadly based Church, where differing insights into the person and teaching of Jesus had been allowed to co-exist.

Unfortunately for those who hold this view, attempts to remake the Early Church in the image of a typical modern denomination suffer from a number of drawbacks which make the total picture seem rather less than convincing. First among these is the notorious dearth of reliable evidence for the origin and development of the first heresies. Our information is invariably filtered through later eyes, much of it is scanty, and no one can say for certain how far imponderable factors, like factional jealousy within a particular congregation, may have influenced the course of events. Undoubtedly the surviving accounts have been distorted by the winning side, though it must be remembered that they are unlikely to be completely fictitious. Beyond that bare minimum, however, we are very largely reduced to speculation.

The difficulty is especially evident in Walter Bauer's major study of the period, *Orthodoxy and Heresy in Earliest Christianity* (*Rechtgläubigkeit und Ketzerei im ältesten Christentum*). Bauer claims that orthodoxy imposed itself gradually on a Church whose more conservative elements, particularly in the non-Hellenic East, strongly resisted it. Unfortunately much of his case rests on evidence culled from the Syriac Church, whose early history is virtually unknown. Bauer makes extensive use of arguments from silence to support his theory, and the result is no more than a possible – and unlikely – reconstruction. Uncomfortable alternatives to his hypothesis are simply brushed aside, and this makes much of his work of questionable value.[38]

Even more serious than this, however, is Bauer's failure to analyse the nature of orthodoxy itself, its coherence as a system, and its obvious appeal to a wide spectrum within the Church. In particular, he cannot explain the extraordinary confidence of the orthodox, not only that their faith was of apostolic origin, but that, if challenged, it would be upheld as such by the broad mass of the Church, especially in the great sees of Antioch, Alexandria and Rome. It can hardly be claimed that the bishops of these sees were in collusion to force their particular policy on the Church; apart from anything else, such an arrangement would rapidly have come unstuck. It is clear that the orthodox were appealing to something deeper and more permanent, to a bedrock of essential truths which the apostolic sees (at least) held in common. In the light of this, Bauer's thesis that orthodoxy was a revolutionary new movement bent on the destruction of primitive pluralism must be regarded as both historically and psychologically improbable.

The question of the apostolic origin of orthodoxy was not tackled by Bauer in any detail, but this lacuna has recently been filled by a young British theologian, James Dunn, in a lengthy and wide-ranging study (*Unity and Diversity in the New Testament*, London, 1977). Dunn's approach is considerably more cautious than Bauer's, but his general outlook is similar. Dunn has clearly been impressed by Bauer's thesis, which he accepts as established fact, though it must be said to his credit that his own study concentrates on the mainstream of evidence represented by the New Testament, and avoids Bauer's dependence on material of dubious value or importance.

But neither Bauer nor Dunn can explain how, if the doctrinal confessions adopted by the Church were mainly philosophical statements, they could appeal to the masses of Alexandria, Antioch and Constantinople, who had never managed to demonstrate a comparable enthusiasm for pagan philosophy. The fact is that, if we are to understand the doctrinal development of the Early Church, we must go beyond the purely intellectual and consider in greater depth the spiritual motives at work.

This task has been greatly facilitated by the Jesuit philosopher and theologian, Bernard Lonergan, whose contribution to religious thought is still not fully appreciated in the English-speaking world. In one of his earliest works, *De Deo trino* (of which the first part has been translated into English, and published as *The Way to Nicea* (London, 1976)), Lonergan describes the development of dogma as the progress from a state of undifferentiated consciousness to a state of differentiated consciousness. At first sight it might seem that as a process of intellectual abstraction, the rise of dogma was indeed a decline, or at least a narrowing, of the primitive faith, and therefore inadmissible. But Lonergan rejects this conclusion by saying that since religion must embrace the whole of human life and experience, it cannot escape the process of differentiation which leads inevitably to the formulation of dogmata.

Lonergan vigorously rejects any suggestion that this process involved the Church in any change in the substance of its belief, or even that it brought about an increase in the clarity of its expression. For him, all that was involved was a movement from one mode of discourse to another, during which the content of scriptural revelation was adapted to the new demands of human consciousness. This development, however, Lonergan distinguishes carefully from any idea of Hellenisation. The Greek philosophers, he insists, were concerned with essences, whereas Christian theologians were preoccupied with what *is*. For them, revealed truth did not merely correspond to reality, as a blueprint corresponds to a building; it *was* reality. This conviction introduced so novel a conception of the relationship between subject and object, thought and thing, God and creation, that it was eventually able to overthrow classical philosophy almost entirely.

Lonergan's analysis is a most interesting and valuable corrective to the usual emphasis in modern studies on the origin of dogma, but there are at least two points at which we must beg leave to dissent from him. Firstly, as Lonergan himself insists,[39] the ante-Nicene writers were unconscious of the development they were furthering, and had they been aware of it, they would have been resolutely opposed. But if this is true, it must make us very cautious of accepting such an interpretation too readily. If we are expected to believe that the early Fathers spent their lives hammering out doctrines in a manner whose implications escaped not only them but all succeeding generations down to the present century, is it not more reasonable to question this modern theory in the light of the ancients' self-understanding? We must be wary of a view which makes so many great thinkers unconscious participants in an historical process beyond their comprehension and contrary to their wishes.

Secondly, it would appear that Lonergan has failed to do justice to the religious character of the Bible as *Scriptura* (*graphē*). In Lonergan's scheme, the Bible is a work of undifferentiated consciousness from which dogmata were extracted according to the evolutionary process we have already described. But Lonergan's claim that the Gospels appeal to the 'whole man' is surely mistaken. A book, by its very nature, speaks primarily to the intellect, and therefore belongs to the sphere of differentiated consciousness. In both Jewish and Christian thought, it was the book which gave impetus to the religion by defining its nature and circumscribing its limits. The disorganised and divided understanding of the pagans was replaced by an integrated world-view in which the intellect (seated in the heart) played the central role. Jewish and Christian religion has always been distinguished by the belief that the Spirit of God speaks through the mind of man to touch and renew the whole of his being.

The power and authority of the written Word bear witness in

themselves to the existence of what Lonergan calls differentiated consciousness, so that the subsequent development of dogmatism is not, properly speaking, the result of a particular mental evolution. The long line of theologians who formulated Christian doctrine were doing no more than setting out the teaching of Scripture in a systematic way. It is certainly true that some were tempted to close the circle, as it were, and offer a fully coherent and logical understanding of God, but in so far as philosophical neatness detracted from some aspect of revelation, it was always repudiated. The mystery of the Godhead could never be fully unveiled to mortal minds, and the orthodox party was always on the alert for any clever addition to the apostolic deposit of truth.

Ancient exegesis has a bad name today because of the way it frequently lapsed into allegory, but this tendency must be understood in its context. The patristic exegetes believed that the clearer passages of Scripture could be used to interpret the more obscure ones, a principle which led them to discover types of Christian doctrine in parables and Old Testament stories. The results were often highly amusing, but as long as this method of interpretation was reserved for tales and legends, it was quite harmless. Allegory became a danger only when it was elevated into a principle by which the whole of Scripture could be interpreted.

The rise of allegory to the key position in biblical exegesis lies outside the scope of this book, but the Early Church's quest for a comprehensive hermeneutical method does not. In many ways it was this problem, and not the more refined questions of trinitarian dogma or christology, which lay at the root of most second-century heresies. The unity of the biblical revelation was challenged by Marcion, who drove a wedge between the creator God (or demiurge) and the redeeming Christ. Marcion interpreted the Pauline antithesis between law and Gospel as licence to dispense with the Old Testament altogether, but Tertullian pointed out, in five long treatises, just how fundamental were the Jewish Scriptures and the Hebraic concept of an omnipotent creator for a proper understanding of Christianity. On a different track, the Valentinians regarded the Bible as a mythical dramatisation of philosophical realities, which they then proceeded to extract from it. The result was

that the historicity of the Bible was played down in favour of
a cosmic hierarchy of personified abstractions like Pleroma
(fullness), Sophia (wisdom) and Nous (mind).

Tertullian attacked these systems by pointing out their internal weaknesses and inconsistencies, but he was not content
to restrict his denunciations to the level of piecemeal analyses
of individual aberrations. He realised that if heresy was to be
combated effectively, it was necessary to expose its roots in a way
of thinking fundamentally alien to the gospel. H. E. W. Turner
has pointed out that Tertullian regarded heresy as a vicious
principle which made use of Scripture texts to lead men astray,
and he contrasts this attitude with the milder judgment of
Origen, according to whom heresy was more usually a right
principle wrongly applied. Stated baldly like this, it would seem
that there is something to be said for each of these views, though
there can be little doubt that it was Tertullian who showed
the deeper insight on this point. Marcion used an essentially
alien conception of what a perfect redeemer should be like in
order to extract him from the Scriptures; as Tertullian pointed
out, an honest reading of the text itself would have led to very
different conclusions. In the same way, the followers of Valentinus regarded their philosophy as the basic reality, and
allegorised the Bible to make it fit.

Against all this, Tertullian argued that Scripture presented its
own world-view which was both consistent within itself (as
opposed to Marcion) and independent of pagan philosophies.
The purpose of Christian doctrinal statements was to elucidate
the teaching of Scripture and safeguard its holiness. The
development of dogma and dogmatism must therefore be seen
as the foundation-stone of the Church's sanctification, since its
purpose was to cleanse the mind from sin. Tertullian was himself fully aware of the dire consequences which would follow
on the abandonment of orthodoxy, and never ceased to dwell
on the intimate connection between mental and moral purity.
In chapter six of his *De praescriptione haereticorum* he reminds his
readers that St Paul himself classed heresy among the *carnalia
crimina* (Gal. 5.20) and he lost no time in pointing out the
ethical deficiencies of Hermogenes (*Adv. Herm.* 1.2) and
Marcion (*Adv. Marc.* i. 1.3–5). He also makes it clear that
immorality is the natural consequence of heresy. A heretic, by

preaching the counsel of an evil spirit, distorts the rule of faith first, and then corrupts moral discipline as well (*De mono.* 2.3).

There can be no minimising the strength and importance of Tertullian's attacks on heresy. To his mind wrong belief was the root cause of wrong behaviour. There can be no more eloquent testimony than this to his belief in the fundamental unity of man in every aspect of his being and existence.

THE SPIRIT AND THE CHURCH

There was one heresy, however, which Tertullian regarded in quite a different light. It may of course be disputed whether or not Montanism was in fact a heresy, since it taught no false doctrines, but the distinction between heresy and schism is hardly more than pedantic in this case. The crisis which the Montanists provoked in the Church had more far-reaching theological implications than that of the Donatists a century and a half later, so that it is misleading to call it a schism. Yet at the same time it did not touch on fundamental trinitarian or christological doctrines as did the clearly defined heresies like Marcionism. But the niceties of these distinctions made little difference in practice. By Tertullian's day the Montanists had been condemned, whether as heretics or as schismatics, and their teaching repudiated both at Rome and in Asia Minor.

Why then did Tertullian approve of the Montanists when he was so disparaging of the other sectarian movements current in his day? The simplest answer, and the one most frequently put forward, is that he was a convert to the sect. This view may be traced back to Jerome and Augustine, and both Neander and Harnack made it a point of central importance. To men of pietistic leanings, the Montanists seemed to be the last of the true, charismatic Christians found in the New Testament, who by this time were being stamped out by an increasingly rigid, ritualistic Catholicism. This was the view of John Wesley, for instance, and it may also be found among modern Pentecostals.[40]

That the pietistic view of Montanism was wide of the mark is now too well established to need refutation. But if Montanism was not the last survival of primitive Christianity, what was it, and why did it attract Tertullian? The facts are not altogether clear, but it seems that somewhere about the year 171 (dates, as usual, being unreliable), three obscure Phrygians began having apocalyptic visions. According to the accounts given by Montanus, Priscilla and Maximilla, the New Jerusalem promised by the Apostle John in his Apocalypse was about to descend at a village by the name of Pepuza. To prepare for this great event, Christians were to sell their belongings, leave their families and congregate near Pepuza to await the promised advent, scheduled for the year 177. Of course nothing materialised, the sect dispersed, and the Church of Asia retaliated with a counter-offensive so sharp at times, that some of its writers apparently even denied the canonicity of the Johannine writings.[41]

But although the sect's raison d'être was soon gone, and the Church was able by and large to restore order in the congregations, the spirit of Montanism did not die so easily. Closely linked with the eschatological visions of the original prophets was a strong emphasis on holiness of life, renunciation of the world and a glorification of martyrdom, for which the Montanists later became famous.[42] They were heavily indebted to the writings of St John, but their real authority came from the sayings of their own prophets. We cannot say whether these were written down by the authors themselves, or copied out by disciples, but it soon became a key element in their teaching that God had inspired the prophet-founders of the sect to carry on the work of revelation accomplished by the Apostles. Even when the initial enthusiasm had died down, these ideas retained their influence, in some places for as much as two centuries and more.[43]

By the time Tertullian encountered it, the movement had already passed through its initial stages and had begun to settle down. It is extremely doubtful whether Tertullian ever met a Phrygian Montanist in the flesh; his first contact with them was most probably through their writings. It is at this point that questions arise. What exactly was Tertullian's relationship to the sect? According to the generally received opinion, Tertullian became a Christian in early manhood, and wrote a number of treatises, including his *Apologeticum* and the first four books of his *Adversus Marcionem* as a loyal if somewhat awkward member of the Great Church at Carthage. As time went on, however, he grew increasingly dissatisfied and adopted an even more radical outlook. Finally about the year 207 he left the Church to embrace Montanism,[44] and under the influence of this movement, wrote the latter part of his work. This general viewpoint has been so widely accepted for such a long time now that even specialist scholars like Frend and Bauer take it for granted.

Unfortunately, however, there is little evidence to support the commonly received account, and it is interesting to note that those who have examined the issue most carefully have usually also been most guarded in their assertion of the traditional theory.[45] As a first point, it seems most unlikely that Tertullian's involvement with Montanism amounted to anything which could properly be called a conversion. For one thing, there is nothing in his writings of the sense of new illumination which conversion brings. The Montanists merely appear in the course of argument where their testimony is used, and that is all. There is no argued apology for the sect, and no attempt to win others to it. In a word, Tertullian *defended* the Montanists; he did not *propagate* their beliefs. This is an important difference, and provides a useful indication of the true nature of his relationship to the Phrygian prophets.

To many, of course, this argument will appear to be mere quibbling over words. Even if the signs of a conversion are lacking, they will argue, Tertullian nevertheless adhered to Montanism as the most congenial expression of his Christian beliefs. This argument rests on a number of considerations, which may be conveniently divided into three main categories: thematic similarities in his work, lexical borrowings, and explicit references. Of the three, only the last is beyond dispute. Yet the astonishing fact is that even here clear, unequivocal references to Montanus, Priscilla and Maximilla are few and far between. There are two instances where all three are mentioned together.[46] Beyond that, Montanus appears once on his own in *De ieiunio* 12.4 and also in *Adversus omnes haereses* 7.2, a work of doubtful authenticity. Prisca, as she was also known, is cited once in *De exhortatione castitatis* 10.5 and again in *De resurrectione mortuorum* 11.2. In sum, therefore, there are four or possibly five treatises out of a total of thirty-one (or thirty-two) in which Montanists are explicitly mentioned. Considering the

THE MAN AND HIS TIMES

great weight attached by scholars to Tertullian's connection with them, this is flimsy evidence indeed. The lexical borrowings of which so much is made are equally unconvincing. The chief examples usually cited are Tertullian's use of the terms *psychicus* (=non-Montanist Christian) and *Paracletus* (=the Holy Spirit). Since both these terms were in common use, in a quasi-technical sense, among the Montanists, it is assumed that Tertullian's use of the terms must reflect a Montanist influence. But does the evidence really stand up? Both words were of course used in the New Testament, and there is no doubt whatever that Tertullian would have expected his readers to hark back mentally to the apostolic teaching quite apart from Montanism. He may well have used them with a note of defiance, to show his sympathies with the sect, but there is no reason to suppose that either he or his readers would necessarily have connected the two. His use of the word *psychicus* in particular demands careful scrutiny. The evidence has been carefully assembled by de Labriolle, who followed Harnack in maintaining that Tertullian had here taken over a typically 'gnostic' term and applied it to the 'catholics'.[47]

De Labriolle saw clearly that *psychicus* in Tertullian could not be divorced from its opposite, *spiritalis*, and that this division had been common in Christian thought from New Testament times. Indeed, St Paul himself distinguished between the *psychikoi* and the *pneumatikoi* at Corinth, and the terms were never in the exclusive possession of off-centre groups on the fringes of the Church. We have already stated our opinion that Harnack (following Neander) made far too much of 'gnosticism' as a phenomenon, and this is a prime example of the kind of distortion which has resulted. As far as Tertullian himself is concerned, there are a great many instances in which *spiritalis* is used without any suspicion of Montanism, and the same is true of *psychicus* in at least three instances.[48] What is interesting, however, and what de Labriolle fails to discuss, is why Tertullian should have used a Greek word for the group he disapproved of, but not for the side he associated himself with. (*Pneumaticus* never appears at all in his work, although there are some instances of *animalis* as the equivalent of *psychicus*.)

The argument that *psychicus* was a technical, gnosticising word sounds plausible enough, until we reflect that it does not really account for Tertullian's preference for *spiritalis* over *pneumaticus* (which on this theory must have been equally technical) or for his occasional use of *animalis*. It seems likely that *psychicus* was indeed meant to convey a special flavour, but not of this kind. In all probability Tertullian originally intended to translate *psychikos* and *pneumatikos* into Latin as part of the common word-stock of early Christian discourse, but ran into difficulty with *psychikos*. *Animalis* is of course the Latin equivalent in so far as *psychē = anima*, but in common usage the Latin word had a rather different meaning from *psychikos*. As everyone knows, *animalis* was usually applied to the lower creation, something which was never true of *psychikos*.[49] The Greek word also had philosophical overtones which could not easily be conveyed by *animalis*. In particular, *psychikos* was used by pagan Greeks of pleasures and pursuits to which the philosophically minded would devote themselves. It was apparently seldom if ever applied to human beings directly, but if it had been, it would scarcely have had a pejorative ring. On the contrary, it would undoubtedly have been almost a pagan equivalent of *pneumatikos*. And this may well have been Tertullian's point. The *psychici* were not bad Christians because they had failed to rise to the higher *gnosis* of the *spiritales*, but because they had allowed their thinking, and consequently also their actions, to be influenced by non-Christian forms of thought. Add to this the note of contempt which the use of a Greek word often conveyed in Silver Age Latin, and we have the perfect description of these people, whose intellectual idolatry was undermining the faith. The use of *psychicus* inc this context may thus be adequately accounted for without recourse to Montanist or 'gnostic' influences.

Closely related to this is the way in which Tertullian uses *nos* and *nostri* when making out his case against the *psychici*. Who is included in this pronoun? Leaving aside the many instances of a purely rhetorical plural, when it is clear that Tertullian really means only himself, we are faced with a number of examples where it would seem that he has drawn a firm line between himself and his like-minded associates on the one hand, and the mass of 'catholic' Christians on the other. But on closer inspection, these examples turn out to be less convincing. As far as *nos* is concerned, we can hardly do better than to quote de

Labriolle himself, who was forced to admit the weakness of his case in many places. As he says:[50]

To tell the truth, *nostri* (*nos, nobis,* etc.) does not always have a 'sectarian' meaning, even in the most definitely Montanist works, and great care is required. Thus, in *De vir. vel.* 17.2, when Tertullian says:, *nobis Dominus etiam revelationibus velaminis spatia metatus est,* he makes no attempt to distinguish his own group from the Catholics, but rather the Catholics – among whom he places himself – from the pagans whose practices he has just cited. In *De mono.* 9, the *nobis* applies to Christians in general, in contrast to the *Romani*; in *Adv. Prax.* 5.5, *in usu est nostrorum per simplicitatem interpretationis* '*sermonem*' *dicere, nostrorum* means either 'our translators' or 'our people' in general (= our brother Christians), or possibly 'the Latins' as against the *Graeci* whom he has just named. In *De pud.* 19.5 it is difficult to decide whether *apud nos* means 'among us Catholics' or 'among us Montanists' though the former is more likely, first because Tertullian had already declared himself to be against heretical baptism in *De bapt.* 15.6, a Catholic treatise, and second, because the same solution was adopted by the Church of Africa in the council held at Carthage around 225.

The last statement in particular makes one question the validity of the traditional interpretation. If *De pudicitia* was a Montanist treatise written (as most authorities hold) around the year 212, and if Tertullian's rigid policy of rejecting heretical baptism was strengthened by Montanist influence, is it likely that a council of the Great Church barely a decade later would have endorsed the well-known views of a notorious schismatic on a matter of such delicacy, without any sort of comment? It is possible of course, but hardly very probable.

De Labriolle further adduces two instances (p. 358) where Tertullian speaks of *vos* and *ecclesiarum vestrarum,* supposedly referring to the members of the Great Church. The first of these is more plausible than the second, but both rest on conjecture. In each case it may be that Tertullian is merely referring to his addressees, and since elsewhere in these same treatises he refers to the *psychici* in the third person (cf., e.g., *De pud.* 10.8), it would seem that they were not intended as a diatribe against them. It is much more likely that Tertullian lived in a situation in which each community had its *spiritales* and its *psychici* without any formal division. Douglas Powell, in a recent article, has defended this view with cogency, maintaining that Tertullian never separated himself from the fellowship of the *ecclesia* at Carthage.[51] On purely lexical and linguistic grounds, therefore, the pro-Montanist case falls flat.

The third and most important line of defence, however, is that Tertullian's later treatises show a strong thematic resemblance to Montanist writings, which indicates that he had been strongly influenced by them. Here we move from questions of form to matters of substance. In particular, three main elements are held to exhibit this continuity of thought. Broadly speaking, they are martyrdom, matrimony and prophecy.

On the first of these, de Labriolle maintains that in *De fuga* Tertullian repents of his earlier leniency towards those who tried to escape death, and invoking the Paraclete, offers a revised and much more stringent interpretation of the duty of martyrdom. But the question immediately arises – where is this more lenient attitude to be found? It is not in *Ad martyras*, a treatise which allows only the strictest course, and praises the fortitude of the condemned in tones which make emulation mandatory. It is not in *Scorpiace* either, which, as we have already mentioned, is if anything even more rigid than *De fuga*. There is a rather backhanded allowance made for it in *Ad uxorem* (i.3.4), though in the context this can hardly be taken as evidence of leniency. The only passage which really supports de Labriolle's argument is *De patientia* 13.6; but even this is not conclusive, since flight in persecution is merely cited as a circumstance, not recommended as a policy.

As far as matrimony is concerned, there is likewise no evidence that Montanism had any effect on Tertullian's views. A comparison of *Ad uxorem* with *De exhortatione castitatis* or with *De monogamia* will readily demonstrate how impossible it is to detect any great shift in Tertullian's attitude. Furthermore, if he did change his mind, it may not have been in the direction of greater intolerance, which the Montanist theory assumes. For example, in *Ad uxorem* i. 1.5 he denies that earthly marriage will exist in heaven, whereas in *De monogamia* 10.5–6 he says that married couples will be reunited in a spiritual union beyond the grave, with the result that a second marriage on earth would be revealed as adultery. This does not really indicate a shift in attitude on Tertullian's part, since the spiritual transformation of marriage rules out any continuation of the earthly institution, but it is remarkable nevertheless that the different emphasis in *De monogamia* has produced a more positive attitude towards matrimony – the very opposite to what one would normally expect from a Montanist.

The subject of prophecy is the most promising of the three topics for those who insist on Tertullian's Montanism, but even here the evidence is rather disappointing. It is true that he does quote Montanist prophecies in a way which seems to give them equality with Scripture, but great caution is required in evaluating his use of them. Tertullian says nothing and quotes nothing which is *distinctively* Montanist; in particular, the descent of the New Jerusalem at Pepuza is never mentioned. What he says about eschatology may have affinities with Montanism, but it is also paralleled in other Christian writers of undoubted orthodoxy, and Tertullian's chiliasm is rather moderate when compared with that of Irenaeus, for example.[52] The ecstatic elements of prophecy were dealt with in *De extasi*, which is now lost, but there is no indication in the surviving literature that Tertullian's interest in them made any difference to his theology. As for the status of the New Prophecy in the Church, von Campenhausen is at pains to point out that the crux of the Montanist heresy was that it accepted the absolute authority of the Montanist revelation, while Tertullian never really agreed to this supersession of the biblical canon.[53] In any case since it was still not clear what the limits of canonical Scripture were, some uncertainty at this point is only to be expected. Tertullian's high view of the prophecies may well have been motivated by a desire to prove that the power of the Holy Spirit had in no way diminished since the time of the Apostles. In any event, this seems to be the thought which lies behind *Passio Perpetuae et Felicitatis*, a contemporary document, also from Carthage.

But the really clinching argument which effectively destroys the notion of thematic continuity, comes when we consider the context of the Montanist quotations. The main interests of the latter were ecstatic, prophetic and eschatological. Tertullian, however, quotes them only when writing on the resurrection of the dead (*De resurr. mort.* 11.2) and on chastity (*De exhort. cast.* 10.5). That there should be several treatises on continence and none recommending prophecy or glossolalia is surely evidence enough of where Tertullian's real interests lay. Even de Labriolle is forced to admit (pp. 299–304) that many aspects of Montanism, in particular the prominent role played by women in the sect, must have been distasteful to Tertullian, whose rigid views on the subject make an obvious contrast. The conclusion is inevitable – Montanism, though it was defended by Tertullian, neither conquered his allegiance nor influenced the development of his thought to any great degree.[54]

But if this is the case, how can we explain Tertullian's positive attitude to the sect? A look at the quotations will quickly tell us the answer, which in any case is obvious. Tertullian backed the Montanists because he saw in them fellow *spiritales*, whose thirst for holiness and concern for discipline equalled his own. Thus we find him quoting Prisca: *sanctus minister sanctimoniam noverit ministrare* (*De exhort. cast.* 10.5) and again: *carnes sunt et carnem oderunt* (*De resurr. mort.* 11.2). In *De pudicitia* 21.8 he uses a Montanist saying to back up his own strict views on church discipline, while at the same time leaving some room, interestingly enough, for the possibility that it may not have been a genuinely prophetic utterance.[55] It is clear, though, that Tertullian's real interest was not in prophecy or eschatology, but in sanctification and discipline. To the extent that the Montanists shared this overriding concern, Tertullian was prepared to welcome them and defend them from attack. Apart from that, he was not interested.

To the weight of internal evidence we may add external considerations as well. Montanus and his disciples were disowned by the Church and their writings burned, whereas Tertullian's survived intact, and he was later regarded as a Father of the Latin Church. It is true that some of his writings, particularly *De extasi*, were not copied in later centuries, but this may have been as much the result of chance as of deliberate policy on the part of the ecclesiastical authorities. After all, if the latter were really trying to destroy all trace of his Montanism, why did they not expurgate treatises like *Adversus Praxean*? And what about the continued survival of *De mono-*

gamia or *De pudicitia*? Clearly nobody felt that these writings were heretical enough to be suppressed, which can only mean that later generations did not take the references to Montanism all that seriously. We suggest that their attitude has much to commend it to us also, and that it is unwarranted to attribute Tertullian's views to the influence of Montanism. Even those aspects of his teaching which strike us as slightly off-beat, e.g. his opposition to digamy, can be supported by numerous parallels in other writers of undoubted orthodoxy.[56] The most reasonable explanation for Tertullian's seemingly eccentric rigorism is also the simplest – above all else he was concerned to do the Will of God in the light of Scripture, and as he says elsewhere, the Will of God is our sanctification (*De exhort. cast.* 1.3).

CONCLUSION

We have now seen that in the main themes which run through Tertullian's writing, the underlying concern, and the one which gives unity to the whole, is the preoccupation with sanctification. For Tertullian, sanctification was the path by which a man might attain to a more perfect knowledge of God. The coming of the Holy Spirit at Pentecost opened up a new dispensation, since it was now possible for the Christian to attain sanctification by the operation of the Paraclete Who dwelt within him (*De mono.* 3.7).

In Tertullian's mind, the work of sanctification was essentially one of restoration, which led eventually to a renewal of life as it was before the Fall (ibid., 17.5). Christ had come, the second Adam, to restore the creation to its primitive state of innocence. Since his ascension, the task had been entrusted to the Holy Spirit who had come to the Church, in accordance with Christ's promise, at Pentecost. This Paraclete – the title served to emphasise the continuity and essential oneness of the Spirit's work with that of Christ – was entrusted with the final perfecting of the restoration, a process whose beginnings could be traced back to Moses and the covenant of Sinai. Through Moses God had revealed the Divine Law which explained the nature and extent of the holiness he required. In its pure form, however, the Law could not be kept without the aid of the Holy Spirit, and so, to ease the burden on the people, God left open certain loopholes. The principles of the Law were of course retained intact; only their application was modified by God's special indulgence (ibid., 14.1, *et passim*). This period of toleration came to an end, however, with Christ. By fulfilling the Law in his life and perfect sacrifice on the Cross, Christ had set the example of holiness in keeping the Law without recourse to God's indulgence. When he had sent the Spirit as Paraclete to empower all men to follow this example, the way was open for the restoration of mankind to its antelapsarian state of innocence.[57]

Tertullian's theological scheme, unlike Marcion's, allowed for successive dispensations in the unfolding of the revelation. But in saying this we must be wary of suggesting that he taught a theory of 'progressive' revelation. 'Progression', in so far as it can be used at all of Tertullian's thought, means only the gradual unveiling of the eternal plan of God, in which the end is a return to the beginning. As with most of the Ancients, he was obsessed with the fear of change. Always his aim was to be more, rather than less, traditional, and any notion of novelty, either in the Paraclete's revelations or in his own arguments, was specifically rejected (*Adv. Prax.* 2.2; *De mono.* 3.2). It would be wrong to regard this protest against novelty as a mere sop to the 'catholics'. On the contrary, it was a basic element in his whole outlook, and one which the world of his day shared. For this reason, his appeals for Christian holiness were justified, not as an advance to a new and higher state, but as a return to the original innocence of man, after which there would be no more falling away (*De pud.* 6.13–18).

It is the purpose of the remainder of this book to examine in detail Tertullian's concept of holiness and how it affected, or ought to have affected, Christian life and discipline. In the next chapter we consider what Tertullian meant by holiness and how he conceived of sanctification. The fourth chapter deals with the acquisition of holiness, in particular, the role of discipline in the light of faith and the authority of Scripture and nature. Finally, we conclude with an examination of how these principles were applied in the test case of matrimony. In the interest of clarity and brevity, we have confined ourselves to the most important feature of Tertullian's asceticism, which

was his emphasis on chastity. It should be borne in mind, however, that the principles enunciated here applied also to other
forms of abstention, especially fasting, with which he also deals.
Throughout, we have endeavoured to emphasise his links with
the mainstream of ancient thought and culture and to show
how closely he depended on them in working out his own
contribution to the ongoing tradition.

CHAPTER THREE

THE NATURE OF
HOLINESS

We have now explained why we believe that it was Tertullian's concern for sanctification which determined his approach to theology and which formed the main theme of his writings. Now we must examine more closely the precise nature of the holiness which he was so intent on securing. At one level, of course, the answer is plain enough. Holiness was the quality peculiar to the very essence of God, and to become holy meant nothing less than to become like God himself. This does not mean that Tertullian was a moralist, at least in the sense in which the word is generally used of philosophers. Surprising though it may seem, ethical behaviour as such held little interest for him, and there are large areas – the whole realm of social ethics, for example – which he more or less ignored. For him the moral imperative was strictly defined in terms of God's character and was dominated by the problem of individual purity. Tertullian's aim was not morality but holiness. But how was this to be worked out in practice? Tertullian believed that man was created in the Divine Image, but how could this be reconciled with the Christian understanding of sin and redemption? Where did sanctification fit in, and how was it to be applied?

These questions cannot be answered without a thorough analysis of Tertullian's anthropology. This is particularly important today when the soundness of his teaching has been widely attacked on the ground that it is both inconsistent with the Bible and irreconcilable with modern thought. With respect to the latter, it may be said at once that Tertullian never considered basing his doctrine of man on what we would call scientific research. This was not simply because many of the tools for such research were not available to him, but also because he regarded biological phenomena as irrelevant to the main issue. His understanding of human physiology was by no means rudi-

mentary, as can be seen from his detailed description of preg-
nancy (cf. *De anima* 25), but at the same time it was ancillary to
his main purpose. Modern theologians who like to claim that
the scientific discoveries of recent years have invalidated
ancient Christian conceptions of man have not understood the
philosophical basis and theological outlook of the Fathers. For
them biology was of passing interest only, and of no importance
in a discussion of human nature. The uniqueness of man lay
not in what united him to the animal creation but in what
distinguished him from it. It was this distinction, however it
may have been defined, which gave to man his special character
as a being created in the image and likeness of God.

This belief is the central fact of Tertullian's anthropology. As
a concept it can be found in Scripture, but the Greek Apologists
of the second century, from whom Tertullian drew much of his
inspiration, had already begun to develop it as a counterpart
– if not quite as a counterweight – to the Platonic conception
of a semi-divine, immortal human soul. In theory the Christian
doctrine of the image and likeness of God embraced the whole
man, but in practice this wider sense was seldom maintained in
the early period, and it would appear that the image was
increasingly identified with the soul (cf., e.g., *Adv. Marc.* ii.5.6).
Unlike Plato, Christian thinkers rooted their exposition of the
divine nature of the soul in the fact that man was a distinct
creation of God, not an emanation from him. The soul's
participation in the Divine was therefore at one remove, and
inferior to the Divine Essence which it reflected. In the Christian
view man's perfection was never autonomous, but only a faithful copy of the character of God. The most important feature of
this was undoubtedly his moral nature, and it was thus that
moral considerations came to play a central part in Tertullian's
teaching about sanctification.

The Christian doctrine of the image and the likeness of God
suffered from a curious semantic difficulty which led the
Apologists to distinguish the image (*eikōn*, *imago*) from the likeness (*homoiōsis*, *similitudo*). This was a distinction unknown in
Hebrew thought, and even Philo, for instance, used the two
words interchangeably.[1] The Greek mind, however, with its
long tradition of philosophical analysis, found it difficult to
accept that the two words could be synonymous. The Greek

Fathers insisted on differentiating the terms and in the process produced a series of inconsistent interpretations which still embarrass Eastern Orthodox theologians.[2] Tertullian inherited something of this confusion, although he apparently worked out one particular understanding of the issue which then served him as his only point of reference.

The variety of possibilities which the Greeks developed provides interesting evidence of how agile they could be in these matters. The Pseudo-Clementine Homilies, for instance, state that while all men are created in the image of God, only the virtuous possess his likeness as well.[3] Irenaeus says much the same thing, although his writings are full of inconsistencies. In one place we read that man was created after both the image and likeness of God (*Adv. haer.* v. 28.4) and – elsewhere – that both were lost at the fall (ibid., iii.18.1). But Irenaeus also says that originally man had neither God's image nor his likeness (ibid., iv.38.3–4). In still another context, he divides these from each other saying that man was created after the image only, and received the likeness by a subsequent operation of the Spirit. At the fall man lost the likeness but not the image (ibid., v.16.1).

Can these inconsistencies in Irenaeus' thought be reconciled? Some have argued that they can, on the ground that the difficulty is purely lexical and does not affect the substance of what Irenaeus believed, which was that fallen man had lost his aboriginal communion with God.[4] This is no doubt correct as far as it goes, but it is hardly a very satisfactory solution. A conclusion as general and obvious as this one may be applied to almost any statement, and it is not sufficient to explain the apparent contradictions. Harnack suggested that Irenaeus was conflating two separate traditions, one of which said that man had been created imperfect, without image or likeness, while the other held that originally human nature must have been perfect. Harnack traced the first of these views to Theophilus of Antioch, the second to St Paul.[5] Such a solution is perhaps possible, but it seems unnecessary to develop a theory of divergent traditions when there is a much simpler solution available. Good Hellene that he was, Irenaeus simply assumed that the image and likeness were different things, but he ran into difficulties when confronted with the ambiguous evidence of Scripture. Since he was not concerned to harmonise his findings, apparent inconsistencies co-exist in his writings but do not affect his basic understanding of the fall. In general, therefore, the traditional commentators are to be preferred to Harnack, but with reservations as to how far the difficulties involved are 'purely lexical'.

Tertullian derived his conception of the image and likeness from Irenaeus, but did not follow any one strand in his thought. Tertullian believed that man was created after both the image and the likeness of God, and that he had lost only the latter at the fall. He therefore accepted the common notion that *image* was a more general term than *likeness*, although the distinction he drew between them is more precise than anything in Irenaeus or Clement of Alexandria (cf. *Strom.* 5.11–12). According to Tertullian, Adam's soul had been created by the breath of the Spirit, and it was this breath which formed the soul's substance (*De anima* 10.1). The soul was therefore of divine origin, but in order to avoid the idea that it was of the same essence as the Divine Nature, Tertullian drew a firm distinction between the Spirit of God as an hypostasis and his breath as a function of this hypostasis. After its procession the breath (*flatus*, *pnoē*) was external to its source and therefore inferior to it (ibid. 11.1). This soul-breath was created in both the image and the likeness of God, and the two had functioned together in harmony before the fall.[6] In so far as it was possible to differentiate between them, the image belonged to the basic nature of man, while the likeness reflected his eternal destiny (*De bapt.* 5.7). Thus when Adam fell he lost the likeness but not the image, which was intrinsic to his nature.

By choosing this interpretation, Tertullian managed to avoid the confusion found in Irenaeus, although there were still potential difficulties in his approach. It is not clear, for example, precisely how the image and the likeness were related to one another. It would seem that the likeness was qualitatively superior to the image in some sense, though apparently it lacked the latter's personal characteristics. Loss of the likeness did not destroy a man's identity as a human being, but loss of the image would have reduced him to animal status. The likeness could only overlay the image and had no truly independent existence. Significantly Tertullian also employed the doctrine of the image to explain the existence of sin. As he understood it, an image, however faithful it might be to its original, was nevertheless still inferior to it, so that the prelapsarian Adam could not claim to be equal with God, although he enjoyed a unique relationship with him. God's moral perfection was part of his immutable nature, but Adam's owed its existence to divine gift (*Adv. Marc.* ii.9.3). In this Tertullian was following Irenaeus as closely as he could; but there was a subtle difference in the way they understood creaturely perfection. For Irenaeus any move away from the essence of God meant a decline in quality, so that human finitude was by definition imperfect and bound to lead eventually to sin. Tertullian, on the other hand, did not adopt this view of necessary evil. For him created perfection had its own real existence and sin was the result of Adam's active disobedience.

This second concept is undoubtedly more in line with St Paul's teaching, but in fact it is very difficult to determine to what extent Tertullian's doctrine genuinely follows the Apostle at this point. One problem is that their interests were somewhat different, so that the degree of overlap between them is surprisingly small, even when it would be most expected. St Paul, for instance, used the doctrine of the creation of man in the image of God to justify the priority of the male over the female, since it was Adam alone who had been created in the image (1 Cor. 11.7). His immediate concern was to justify the veiling of women, and it was in this context that Tertullian used the passage, though he did not go into an explanation of the meaning of the image (*De vir. vel.* 7.2; 8.1). No doubt this was fair enough, but it shows either that Tertullian saw no necessary connection between St Paul's disciplinary advice, in which he was chiefly interested, and the ontological issue on which it was based, or that if he did, he did not think it important enough to discuss. In the same way, although he said a good deal about Christ as the Second Adam, he did not stress the image of God motif in his christology to anything like the extent to which St Paul did.

It seems quite clear that there is a considerable difference of emphasis here between Tertullian and St Paul, but it is much harder to say just how significant this difference is in practice. It is in fact precisely because the Second Adam motif was basic to Tertullian's Christology that he said little or nothing specific-ally about the image of God in Christ. For if Christ was the Second Adam, it followed logically that he must conform in every respect to the first Adam. Thus whatever might be said about the first Adam would apply automatically to Christ as well. It was therefore more important to determine the nature of the first Adam and let the Second fit in accordingly. This was the logic which enabled Tertullian to link the incarnation with the creation of the world, and so present Christ as the key to *anakephalaiōsis*, or recapitulation, which was the essence of his eschatology as it was also of the Apologists. It will be seen at once that this idea is akin to the Stoic belief in the renewal of the cosmos, and there is little doubt that Stoicism was an influential factor in determining the development of the early Fathers' eschatology. This does not mean, however, that either they or Tertullian were Christian Stoics, or that the ontological motifs inherent in a doctrine of recapitulation cannot be found in St Paul's thought as well.

In fact, as Herman Ridderbos has recently reminded us, there is much to indicate that St Paul too regarded Adam and the creation order as fundamental to any discussion of the image of God in Christ. It is true that some scholars have denied any such connection, but as Ridderbos has convincingly shown, St Paul not only regarded Adam's humanity as the prototype of Christ's, he also spoke of the image of God in Christ in the context of creation.[7] The close similarity between the Apostle and Tertullian is even clearer if we compare their views with Philo's, for example. Philo held that in the Genesis account there was a parallel creation of a heavenly man alongside the earthly Adam, and various attempts have been made to connect this opinion with some of St Paul's teaching. But while there may be superficial resemblances between the 'heavenly man' of Philo and the 'heavenly man' of St Paul, it is obvious that the Apostle could never have adopted Philo's concept whole-sale. To have done so would have meant denying the humanity of Christ in the descent of Adam. It would also have implied that ordinary men were sinful in virtue of their earthly nature and not by a free exercise of the will. On both these points, the views of St Paul and of Tertullian are so close as to be virtually identical, and there is no reason to suppose that Tertullian was not copying his mentor faithfully on this point.

An even more important similarity between the Pauline doctrine of the image and Tertullian's teaching is the strong emphasis both place on its moral significance. St Paul's position is made quite clear in a passage like Colossians 3.10, which in the words of Gerhard Kittel '. . . show us once more how slight is Paul's interest in mythical speculation and how strong is his concern for the supremely concrete ethical consequences of this restoration of the *eikōn*, namely, that we should put off fornication, blasphemy and lying'.[8] Apart from Kittel's use of the word *eikōn* (instead of *homoiōsis*), Tertullian could not have agreed more.

At the same time, however, there were important differences between Tertullian and St Paul and these had far-reaching consequences. We have already traced the development in post-biblical thought of an artificial separation between the image and the likeness of God. The practical effect of this was that it blurred the sharp contrast which St Paul had made between the fallen Adam and Christ. For him the restoration of the image of God in man entailed a radical transformation which could appropriately be described in terms of a new birth and a new nature. But Tertullian held that fallen man retained the image. Therefore restoration, because it involved a restoration of the likeness only, was no longer primarily a transformation but a completion or perfection of what was already there in essence (cf. *De exhort. cast.* 1.3).

The difficulty was compounded by an inevitable tendency to hypostatise the image of God, in practice if not specifically in theory. Had Tertullian been content to interpret the image of God in spiritual and moral terms only, he might have avoided some of the more serious problems. But this was hardly a viable option, since it would have given the impression that the image of God was purely fictitious. To men trained in Stoicism, it seemed obvious that existence required hypostatisation for it to have any meaning at all. This idea is not found in St Paul's teaching, but would not necessarily have contradicted it, provided that the hypostatised image were no longer present in fallen man. But this is precisely what Tertullian refused to admit, with the result that for all practical purposes the image of God in man was assimilated to the soul in its fallen state.

Against those who would dispute this conclusion we would urge the following points. The image possessed all the characteristics of the *animal rationale*, including the essential element of free will (*Adv. Marc.* ii.6.3). Like the soul, which needed the Spirit to establish its communion with God, the image too was incomplete without the addition of the likeness. Furthermore, both the soul and the image were of divine origin, and both had lost their faculty for communion with God at the fall. Now Tertullian was concerned, as we know, with the restoration of the likeness to the image of God in man (*De exhort. cast.* 1.3). But if this likeness bore the same relationship to the image as the Spirit to the soul, if indeed the two things were identical, then we should expect the restoration of the likeness to occur by an outpouring of the Spirit on the soul. And of course this is precisely what we find. Tertullian's pneumatocentric theology was not the product of a diluted Montanism, but the logical consequence of his whole approach.

In Tertullian's thought, therefore, the image of God may be identified with the soul for all practical purposes. This conjunction played an important role in his theology, a point of even greater significance when we remember that it was here that he differed most seriously from the thought of St Paul. The result was that although both men emphasised many of the same things, particularly the moral imperative bound up with sanctification, Tertullian's application necessarily proceeded along different lines. Whether in the end this produced a form of Christianity incompatible with the New Testament, or whether the common aim of sanctification was able to override the differences of approach, is the question we must seek to answer in the following pages.

THE SOUL

The best place to begin a discussion of Tertullian's anthropology is undoubtedly with the soul. Tertullian wrote at least three treatises on it, of which two survive,[9] and the subject frequently recurs in his writings. Furthermore, his doctrine of the soul has been the subject of intensive research, although on the whole this has been done by a few dedicated individuals who have devoted themselves exclusively to the subject, and it has not become a matter for general speculation.[10] It is probably fair to add that most of the work which has been done in the field, though in many ways exhaustive, has concentrated heavily on philosophical questions and ignored the implications of the doctrine for Tertullian's theology.

The main outline of Tertullian's doctrine can be stated briefly. He believed, in common with most schools of thought at the time, that the soul was of divine origin (*De anima* 11.1; *Apol.* 17.6), although not in the Platonic sense, since it was not impassible (*De anima* 24.1; cf. *De resurr. mort.* 17.2). Like Philo and many others, he taught that the soul had originated when the Spirit of God breathed his *flatus* (*pnoē*) into the clay corpse of Adam. As we have already seen, however, this *flatus* was only a product of the Spirit and therefore inferior to him in essence. The soul was endowed with both a mind and emotions, and it is significant that Tertullian believed that these were both equally subordinate to it (*De anima* 18). The seat of the soul (a question much discussed in antiquity) was the heart, a belief which Tertullian could support without difficulty from Scripture (ibid., 15).

The soul was by nature simple, indivisible, and entirely rational (ibid., 16.1). It was also corporeal (*De resurr. mort.* 17.2), an idea which has caused much scandal. In fairness, however, it must be said that much of this reaction, as Augustine pointed out, has been due to a misunderstanding of Tertullian's terminology, so that it is not altogether illuminating to call him a 'materialist' as some have unfortunately done.[11] It would be better to say that for him the soul was a solid substance which consequently retained its shape outside the body. This was Tertullian's main interest, which is not at all the same as saying that the soul would have been visible by mechanical means, like a superfine microscope. Tertullian *may* have believed something of the kind, and he certainly did think that the soul was in some sense visible, but we must be careful not to press this into a crude chemical analysis of his teaching. The soul's visibility was not of the ordinary kind (*De anima* 8–9) and there is no mention of the soul-substance as a fifth element, as was sometimes taught in Middle Platonism.[12]

The creation of the individual soul was coincident with the moment of conception, and Tertullian explains that it was not a special gift from God but part of the natural process of birth (ibid., 19). Likewise, soul and flesh matured together through adolescence, each substance developing the elements peculiar to its nature. At death the soul left the body, not in stages but at a particular moment, and it would be reunited with the flesh at the final resurrection (*De resurr. mort.* 28.6).

The most important part of Tertullian's teaching on the soul, however, concerned the nature of its fall into sin. He could not accept the Platonic idea that the soul was imprisoned in a mortal (sinful) body of flesh, and argued that the true cause of the fall was the disobedience of the will which was a part of the soul itself (*Adv. Marc.* ii.5.5). In other words sin was not onto-logically bound up with the nature of flesh, but accidental, and ultimately more the fault of the soul.

Stated simply like this, Tertullian's doctrine of the soul seems straightforward and logical enough. Its affinities with the New Testament teaching, however, and even more, its possible rela-tionship to modern thought, are much more difficult questions, complicated by the fact that Tertullian was forced to work out his ideas against a background of philosophical speculation, most of which is now discredited. By no means all scholars would agree that Tertullian was attached to a particular philo-sophical system; indeed, the majority would probably incline to the view that he was at least eclectic and often fiercely anti-philosophical, however much philosophy in general may have influenced his way of thinking. But we believe that this view, while certainly not without merit, approaches the issue in the wrong way and leads to unnecessary confusion. Tertullian regarded philosophy as an accessory to theology and used it accordingly. But although many of his words were borrowed from the philosophers, the spirit in which he wrote was quite different, and it was this which in the end was more important.

To measure the impact which pagan philosophy had on Tertullian's thought, we must take a brief look at the main currents with which he had to deal. The first of these was Platonism. It was Plato more than any other philosopher who fixed the doctrine of the soul at the centre of philosophical speculation. By Tertullian's time primitive Platonism had evolved and diversified itself, but the main outlines remained recognisably the same (cf. *De anima* 23–4). In Platonic thought the soul was at once both antithetical to the forms and of the some order. The soul was the knower, the forms were the objects known. Individual souls were divine, immaterial, pre-existent and immortal. They were parts of one soul-substance and in absolute terms were infinitely more real than the bodies through which they passed in successive incarnations. Because the soul was divine, it was aware of everything that existed. Plato could not believe that the incarnated soul acquired any genuine knowledge through the bodily senses, so he was obliged to develop a doctrine of anamnesis, or recollection, which meant that the soul learned by recalling truths which it had temporarily forgotten. This idea, like that of transmigration, was not popular with everything, but it remained generally characteristic of Platonism as a school of thought.

The soul was the link between form and matter. A world-soul existed which ordered the *kosmos* in the same way that the individual soul ordered the microcosmic human being. Plato occasionally spoke of the soul as a unity (cf. *Phaedo.* 64 ff.), but in his more developed thought, especially in the *Republic*, he analysed it into three parts which he called *to logistikon* (rational), *to thymoeides* (passionate) and *to epithymētikon* (concupiscent) (*Resp.* 439e). Later systematisations of his thought modified these to *to logikon* (apparently first used by the Stoic Zeno, *Stoic.* 1.1.15), *to thymikon* (a word used, by Plato elsewhere) and *to epithymētikon*. Following their master Plantonists regarded the *logikon* (sometimes identified with the *nous*) as the ruling element in the soul (*to hēgemonikon* in Stoic parlance) and said that it was supported in its efforts by the *thymikon*. Working together these two could subdue the *epithymētikon*, which Plato thought was the seat of evil in the soul. But it was not altogether clear precisely how the *thymikon* differed from the *epithymētikon*. As their names suggest, both were connected with *thymos* (passion) and as such shared a common opposition to the *logikon* within the soul. Plato did his best to distinguish them, but it cannot be said that his efforts were very successful.

Very different from the Platonic conception was Aristotle's definition of the soul. As a system of thought Aristotelianism never really got off the ground in antiquity, but Aristotle himself was too important to be ignored. It has not been possible to prove that Tertullian was directly influenced by him,[13] but indirect influences abound, mediated for the most part through Stoicism. For Aristotle, the relationship between the soul and the body was the same as that between form and matter. The soul was not a separate substance united with the body as in Plato's thought, but the shape in which the bodily matter was structured in the living organism. To him the human soul was the apex of a hierarchical structure of life which embraced animals and plants as well. In this respect it seems that he was prepared to connect *psyche* with the more general *pneuma*, particularly the *symphyton pneuma* which he regarded as especially characteristic of animals.[14] The distinction which Aristotle drew between them was that *pneuma* was always a general term, whereas *psyche* was individualised. There is no instance in which man is said to possess *pneuma* (still less *a pneuma*). The soul of man is always distinguished as *psyche*, occasionally with the addition of a qualifying adjective like *noetike*, to indicate that it alone had the divine quality of *nous* or *logos*.[15] Tertullian, however, rejected the idea that the human soul was essentially the same as animal or plant life. He regarded man as a separate creation and repudiated the suggestion that he could be reduced to animal (or vegetable) status by the removal of certain distinguishing characteristics (*De anima* 19).

The third important school of thought for our purposes was the Stoic. There is no doubt that Tertullian sympathised with the Stoics more than with Plato or Aristotle, so much so that some have thought that he was a Stoic himself. That, however, is going too far. Tertullian undoubtedly found Stoicism congenial in many respects, but he always kept his distance from it and never tried to make St Paul over into a Stoic in the way that Philo, for instance, endeavoured to show that Moses had really been a Middle Platonist.[16]

Stoic psychology combined Platonic and Aristotelian elements and grafted them on to a view of the universe which was essentially pre-Socratic. From Plato there came the idea of the soul's immortality, though in a modified form. The Stoics attributed immortality (like pre-existence) not to the individual soul but to the soul-substance, the divine fire or *pneuma* out of which the individual soul sprang. Also Platonic was the idea that the soul was rational, although again the Stoics saw this in a different light. For them the soul had no element of irrationality whatever, except in so far as it had been corrupted. The *thymikon* and the *epithymētikon*, therefore, had no right to exist and the wise man, in his quest for perfect Apathy, was expected not merely to control but to erase these alien elements in his soul.

From Aristotle the Stoics borrowed the concept of the soul and body subsisting in the relationship of form to matter, but their cosmology prevented them from adopting this idea in pure form. Since the Stoics, unlike Plato or Aristotle, were complete materialists, they could not accept that the soul was anything other than a body. To insist on two separate substances could only weaken the concept of unity held by Aristotle, but the Stoics did their best to overcome this problem. They replaced the form and matter analogy with active and passive principles, which combined to form objects discernible to the senses. The active principle in man was his soul, the passive principle was his flesh. Both were corporeal substances and therefore separable, but in a living man the soul was perfectly diffused through the body and the two formed a harmonious working unity.

By Tertullian's time the great age of Stoic philosophy was already past, although this was not yet generally apparent to contemporaries. Platonism, on the other hand, was in a continuing ferment which in the next century would flower in the work of Plotinus and his disciples. Tertullian sensed this new movement and it is no accident that so much of his *De anima* is taken up with a detailed refutation of Plato. His Stoic leanings are apparent, and at one point he was even able to claim Seneca as *saepe noster*, so close had he been to Christianity at many points (*De anima* 20.1). But interesting as this is, its importance should not be exaggerated. When we inspect their respective teachings more closely, we shall discover that Tertullian in fact completely inverted Stoic doctrine and created from it a new synthesis based not on pagan speculation, but on the revelation of God in Scripture.

It would be simplistic and misleading to suggest that Tertullian used the Scriptures as his textbook in a way similar to that in which pagans used their favourite philosopher's writings. For him the Bible was important not just because he was a Christian, but because its words had been given by God himself and were therefore solid and objective truth, whereas the pagan writings, however noble and exalted, were only human opinion. This difference was decisive. A man like Seneca might share Christian ideas and attitudes to some extent, but this was due to his extraordinary ability to understand general revelation, which was not enough to be saved. Only the Bible contained final truth, because it alone was the direct revelation of God to men. It is interesting that Tertullian says little or nothing about critical problems in Scripture; the matter seems not to have disturbed him at all. Probably the main reason is that attacks on the truth of Scripture, when they came, were from pagans and sceptics outside the Church, intellectuals who in Tertullian's day ignored the Word altogether (*De test. an.* 1.4).

Tertullian believed that Scripture, and the Person of Jesus Christ whom Scripture revealed as the Son of God, were the determining factors in all philosophical and theological construction. We may think it somewhat surprising that he should have used the story of Dives and Lazarus to prove that the soul was corporeal (*De resurr. mort.* 17), but on reflection this is not to be wondered at. After all, the parable does presuppose that there is such a thing as a sensible post-mortal existence, which is what Tertullian was trying to assert. It is true of course that the issue of the soul's corporality arose in the first instance out of philosophical speculation, not scriptural exegesis, but this does not necessarily mean that Tertullian's mistake led him into error. His main point was to establish the reality of post-mortal existence, and there is no doubt that the parable lends support to this idea. What is important to notice here is that it was the scriptural testimony which decided the issue in favour of the Stoics, not the other way round. On its own merits the doctrine would not have gained such a ready hearing, and had any passage of Scripture contradicted it, Tertullian would certainly have repudiated it.

It will be noted here that Tertullian's method was to take an already existing idea, compare it with Scripture, and then modify or abandon it according to the biblical evidence. He knew of course that the Bible had an inner logic of its own, but in his apologetic technique he seldom bothered to develop this beyond the universally accepted *regula fidei* (see the next chapter). In general, when faced with a philosophical problem, he preferred to adapt already existing concepts to accord with Christian teaching. This was all right so long as Scripture made it clear why and how a given concept had to be modified. When no such guidance was forthcoming, however, or when the evidence was ambiguous, Tertullian would often keep to the pagan notion, especially if some superficial support could be found for it. It was for this reason that he never abandoned his concept of the soul and flesh as two distinct, though co-operating substances. Both terms occurred in Scripture, but their precise relationship depended on the inner logic of Hebraic anthropological thought and was never clearly spelled out. Tertullian therefore retained the notion of two substances, fully persuaded that nothing in the Bible contradicted this understanding, even though he frequently modified the precise nature of this distinction when the Scriptures evidently made this necessary.

Tertullian's use of Scripture to judge philosophy is well illustrated by his treatment of the rational and irrational elements in the human soul. Like the Stoics Tertullian believed that the soul was simple and entirely rational, though his reasons for saying this were different from theirs. Tertullian's model was not a theoretical wise man but the real incarnate God. The Stoics were wrong to say that the passions were irrational (and therefore evil) because Jesus, who was both entirely rational and sinless, had passions like those of other men (*De anima* 16.3–5). Tertullian's refusal to analyse the soul in the Stoic manner was a revolution of fundamental importance, because it transcended the dualism latent in Hellenistic culture and made it untenable. Even the preservation of the distinction between the soul and the flesh, which many would say was the essence of dualism (at least in the thought of this period), cannot overrule this basic fact. The flesh after all was only disapproved of because, like the passions of the soul, it was irrational (sinful). Jesus, however, as perfect God and perfect man, had human flesh as well as a complete soul, which automatically removed the theoretical basis of an ontological dualism in human nature such as the Stoics and the Platonists held.

Against the ontological (and therefore necessarily fatalistic) conception of evil implied in Stoic psychology, Tertullian argued that the presence of evil in the soul was accidental and voluntary. Man had turned from good to evil by the exercise of his free will, and as a result the devil had corrupted the entire soul, irrespective of its various 'parts'. The Stoics sought purification in a state of Apathy, which meant the suppression of the 'lower' parts of the soul (not to speak of the flesh) by the 'higher' part. But for Tertullian such a procedure was illusory. For the soul to achieve purification it had to be completely transformed.

It is essential that we keep this doctrine of the soul's corruption in the proper tension with the teaching on recapitulation which we outlined earlier. Tertullian did not believe that sin was a mere deprivation, the removal of the likeness. Inherent in his doctrine was the notion of human guilt, which stemmed from the disobedience of the will as the First Cause of original sin. The foundations of the later Augustinian doctrine were already laid by Tertullian in this way. It is he who deserves the credit for seeing the importance of the will for Christian faith, and it is his insight here as much as anything which rescued Western Christianity from the ontological conception of evil which has exerted such a powerful influence in the Eastern tradition.[17]

When we attempt to compare Tertullian's doctrine of the soul with New Testament teaching, however, we encounter serious difficulties. For in the strict philosophical sense, the New Testament, and the Pauline corpus in particular, contains no doctrine of the 'soul' at all. In keeping with Hebrew tradition, St Paul used both 'soul' and 'flesh' as metaphors for man in his earthly existence, so that far from being antitheses they appear to overlap in meaning, particularly when used adjectivally. Here St Paul was genuinely conservative, reflecting the Old Testament pattern even in preference to ideas current in contemporary Judaism. This point was emphasised by Robert Jewett, who after a major study of the Apostle's anthropological terms, concluded as follows:

Psychē [sc. in St Paul] is used for the most part with one of three basic connotations, all of which stem from Old

Testament usage. It can bear the sense of one's earthly life as it is publically [*sic*] observable in behaviour; the sense of the individual's earthly life which can be lost in death; or the sense of the individual person. The particular sense of the word depends upon the context in which it is used rather than upon a development within Paul's thought. From the first to the last letter, Paul remains basically within the Judaic tradition at this point. There are, however, several connotations of *psychē* within popular Judaic usage which Paul appears to avoid. He never uses it in the strict sense of the 'soul', i.e. the God-related portion of man which survives after death. Furthermore, Paul avoids the interchangeability between *pneuma* and *psychē* which was the mark of Rabbinic usage, related as it was to the question of the soul after death.[18]

Jewett goes on to point out that the adjectives *psychikos* and *sarkikos* (or *sarkinos*) are both predicated of fallen man in the New Testament, and their virtual synonymity at this point is now widely accepted. How far Tertullian understood this is hard to say. Oddly enough, it is his use of *carnalis*, rather than that of *animalis* or *psychicus*, which is the chief cause of our uncertainty. The latter term frequently bears its Pauline sense in Tertullian, but the former is conspicuous by its relative absence. The only instance in which *carnalis* undoubtedly bears its biblical meaning is in a direct quotation from 1 Corinthians 3.1 (*De praescr. haer.* 27.4). Otherwise it seems that Tertullian avoided applying the word to people, except in its adverbial form (cf., e.g., *De resurr. mort.* 11.1).

The reasons why Tertullian was apparently reluctant to use *carnalis* in what to us is its most familiar meaning, remain somewhat mysterious. The possibility of a Montanist influence may be discounted straightaway (cf., ibid., 11.2). It is much more likely that Tertullian realised that the two words overlapped in meaning, but that he avoided *carnalis* as much as possible for tactical reasons. Since he lived in a philosophical climate which tended to exalt the soul and despise the flesh, he was concerned to ensure that the latter would be given its due honour in Christian teaching. We can therefore understand why he chose to avoid a term which might so easily have detracted from this aim. As for the apparent synonymity between *carnalis* and *psychicus*, Tertullian would not have found this at all unusual. The soul and the flesh worked together in perfect harmony and shared responsibility for moral failure. It was not inconceivable that the two words should appear to overlap in meaning at this point, and Tertullian had no difficulty integrating this apparently curious phenomenon into the broader pattern of his thought.

SOUL AND FLESH

There would appear to be little doubt that the close co-operation which Tertullian envisaged between the soul and the flesh was the direct result of his understanding of the New Testament. It is true that his conceptual framework, in which soul and flesh were two distinct substances had more in common with ancient philosophy than with St Paul, but it would be a mistake to regard it as dualistic. Physically, logically and ethically the two substances co-operated so closely that the theoretical distinction between them became largely irrelevant in practice. The theoretical basis for this understanding was of course the incarnation of Christ.[19] In the Old Testament there were recorded numerous instances of prophets and others whose soul had been captured by the Spirit of God, but none of these examples was in any way the equivalent of a divine *enfleshing*. It was this factor which made all the difference, for it proved that the flesh as well as the soul partook of God's redemptive activity.

The earthly life of Jesus, moreover, was the perfect prototype of the life to which the Christian should aspire. Tertullian interpreted the *imitatio Christi* in terms of complete obedience to the Will of God in a way which naturally included the flesh as well as the soul. In practice this meant a moral imitation of Jesus' earthly life – Tertullian was never so crude as to suggest that every Christian should become an itinerant healer and preacher. In fact he based his interpretation of the *imitatio* on the example set by St Paul. It is true that he never quoted the Apostle's famous dictum, 'Be imitators of me, as I am of Christ' (1 Cor. 4.16), but he did insist that Christians owed their spiritual birth to the Apostle (*De mono.* 6.1; *Adv. Marc.* v.7.2;

8.5) and the practical effect was the same. If St Paul was the Christian's father-in-God, then it was only right that his precepts and example should be followed by the children. This line of reasoning was especially applicable to the controversial subjects of matrimony and sexual relations, as we shall see.

The inclusion of the flesh in redemption raised a whole series of problems concerning the means by which the desired end would be achieved. In particular Tertullian had to show how an earthly substance, however much it might be purified, could participate in a heavenly salvation. He perceived that this could be done only by forging a link between the soul and the flesh so strong that it would be impossible even to contemplate the salvation of the one without the other. For the sake of convenience it is probably easiest to analyse his understanding of the union of the two substances according to the categories of ancient philosophy (physics, ethics, logic), though it must be remembered that he himself used these categories very loosely, if at all, in his thinking, and there is certainly no exposition of the union along such rigid lines in his writings.

The physical unity of the soul and the flesh was expressed in terms of a shared life-cycle. Both substances came into being at conception and both grew to maturity together. The soul had no independent pre-existence, nor was it infused into the flesh at birth (cf. *De anima* 25). These factors, especially when they are considered in the light of Tertullian's concern to establish a complete equality between soul and flesh, make it probable that he believed that both substances were transmitted by natural procreation. This would also explain how Adam's sin was imputed to his descendants, something which would have been impossible on the theory that each soul came directly from God. There was also the further consideration that soul and flesh would overcome the separation of death and be reunited at the resurrection. There was thus no possibility of transmigration or metempsychosis, ideas which Tertullian rejected with scorn (ibid., 28–33). At the same time, of course, he agreed that the reconstitution of the human body at the resurrection would not simply mean a return to the mortal state. In the new creation flesh and soul would both be changed into the likeness of Christ's glorified body, which meant that they would be perfected without a change of substance (*De resurr. mort.* 55–6).

When pressed to explain this doctrine in the light of St Paul's teaching that flesh and blood would not inherit the Kingdom of God (ibid., 50), Tertullian retorted with a twofold answer. On the one hand, it was a mistake to identify the resurrection with the Kingdom, which was spiritual in nature,[20] and on the other hand, the passage referred not to the substance of the flesh but to its works (De carn. Chr. 16; De resurr. mort. 49). This in fact was the standard line Tertullian used to explain every instance in the New Testament where 'flesh' implied a principle which was in active opposition to the Spirit (cf. De resurr. mort. 45–6). The works of the flesh were not dependent on its nature but on the activity of the (fallen) soul from which they originated. Thus he came close to using 'flesh' in these passages as a metaphor for man's earthly being, so that in practice there was little difference between him and St Paul on this particular point.

The logical union of the soul and the flesh is less obviously central to Tertullian's doctrine; indeed, it was this aspect which subsequently gave rise to the greatest difficulties; but it is not hard to see why Tertullian felt it necessary to insist on it along with the rest. Formal logic was a powerful ingredient in all ancient thought, and he could not leave such an obvious loophole for those who wished to downgrade the flesh. But in this instance it was the soul, not the flesh, which was forced downwards, at least from the standpoint of Platonism. Tertullian's argument was that if the flesh was a body (corpus) in full union with the soul, then the soul must likewise be a body, coterminous with that of the flesh. Here it was Stoic doctrine which came to his aid, as we have already seen. It is important to emphasise that the corporality of the soul was a logical concept, not a physical one. Tertullian was fully aware that the properties of the soul-body were quite different from those of the flesh-body, and he wished to insist only that their organisational structure as substances was identical (De anima 5–8). We cannot therefore interpret his belief in the corporality of the soul as 'materialism' in any of the usual senses of that word.

Tertullian doctrine of the unity between soul and flesh reached its highest peak of development on the ethical plane. Physics and logic prepared the ground for ethics by ensuring that neither substance could act independently of the other. It is true that Tertullian had to modify this idea slightly to accommodate the behaviour of the disembodied soul, but this did not destroy the principle that the soul could only suffer or act effectively by means of the flesh (*De resurr. mort.* 17). Without it the soul's sin could never have come to realisation. Likewise, without the soul to inform it, the flesh would have had no conscious knowledge of sin at all. The guilt for sin was borne by both substances in equal measure according to their respective natures. It was through the weakness of the flesh that sin gained access to the soul, therefore it was the flesh which bore the responsibility for putting the soul into mortal danger. But it was the will of the soul which had chosen to sin and had used the flesh to carry out its purpose. Responsibility was therefore shared, but since ultimately sin was an act of the will and not the inevitable result of fleshly weakness, the weight of the burden fell on the soul. Redemption could thus hardly be confined to the soul since it was because of it that the flesh had been led into sin in the first place (*De anima* 40). If the soul, as the greater culprit, could be redeemed, it followed that the flesh also must enjoy the possibility of salvation. It is entirely wrong to suppose that Tertullian's view of redemption was superficial or legalistic, a matter of suppressing the sins of the flesh only. He fully understood that salvation was a work of divine grace which purified both soul and flesh together.

By raising the flesh to the level of the soul (or perhaps more accurately, by lowering the soul to the level of the flesh), Tertullian virtually abolished the antithetical relationship between them which was such a common feature of classical philosophy, and thus laid the foundation for its eventual overthrow. It is important to remember, however, that this radical restructuring of the link between soul and flesh was not the result of extended reflection but rather the product of intense theological controversy. At stake was the whole nature of the Christian revelation, as opposed to the pagan philosophies of his time. The first half of the second century was a period of rapid intellectual development within the Greek-speaking Church, and many efforts were made to construct a *modus vivendi* between the Christian faith and Hellenistic philosophies. Not all of these attempts were heretical but the fledgling theo-

logical structure of the Christians found it difficult to cope with
the advanced subtleties of philosophical speculation, and it was
not long before prominent intellectuals in the Church were
adopting the latter as a basis on which to restructure what to
them was still a fundamentally alien theology.

It is now customary to lump these tendencies together under
the catch-all heading 'gnosticism', but this title is misleading
for several reasons. It suggests an inner unity of thought
between the various systems which did not exist, and it tends to
overlook the fact that there was a perfectly orthodox form of
gnosis which was never condemned by the Church. There is no
indication that the early Christians regarded rational thought
as intrinsically heretical, and Harnack's well-known theory that
dogmatic development was a deviation from the original faith
has no foundation in fact.[21] What opposition there was to
philosophy was not directed against logical definitions of what
was (supposedly) incomprehensible, but against attempts to
construct a system of thought in which Christian elements
were either subordinated to alien presuppositions or re-
interpreted in the light of them.

The first Christian writer to undertake a systematic refutation of these heresies was Irenaeus, and his work remains a
primary source of information about them. Irenaeus endeavoured to prove that heresy was a phenomenon as old as the
Church itself, and that it had been combated by the Apostles
from the beginning (*Adv. haer.* i.23.1). He was quite certain
that heresies were due to a refusal to accept the Apostolic
teaching which had been handed on in the churches of
Apostolic origin and was contained in their authentic writings
(ibid., iii.1–5). This refusal had led to many deviations, of
which the most serious were those which attacked the biblical
doctrine of creation. Irenaeus firmly rejected dualistic systems
which tried to explain the existence of evil by postulating
another creator or source of being apart from the infinite Good.
According to him all created things, good or bad, had their
origin in the one Creator, who was himself entirely good.

This of course left Irenaeus with the problem of the origin
of evil. If God could not engender something contrary to his
nature, where had evil come from? As we have already seen,
Irenaeus answered that the root of evil was contained in the

nature of creation itself. A created substance was of necessity inferior to its creator, and was therefore inherently imperfect in relation to him. But no imperfect being could successfully imitate a perfection which was beyond it; hence man as a creature was virtually bound to sin from the start (ibid., iv.38.1). The glory of the Christian revelation was that God himself, by becoming incarnate in a human body, divinised human nature and enabled it to conquer death. The life of Christ was extended by baptism in the Holy Spirit to all men who would receive it, and this baptism was the initiation into the life of grace which communicated the firstfruits of divinity to the soul (ibid., v.6.1; 9.1). In this way the image of God in man was progressively restored into that perfect likeness of the Father which was Christ.

Tertullian adopted the basic outline of Irenaeus' teaching, but developed it in a different direction. He agreed that the possibility of man's sinning derived from his inferior status as a creature, but he did not connect this with a Platonic doctrine of perfection. Adam was not only good by nature at his creation, but he was also perfect and under no compulsion, however indirect, to commit sin. His disobedience in the garden was entirely an act of free will, which brought guilt and death on him and on his descendants. The incarnation of Christ broke this entail of sin not merely in ontological terms (i.e. Jesus was the Second Adam, the perfect man), but in juridical ones as well. By his sacrifice on the cross the Son of God paid the penalty of sin and purchased our redemption by his blood (cf., e.g., *De fuga* 12.3).

It is sometimes said that Tertullian had no real doctrine of the atonement and that the significance of this act escaped his notice.[22] This opinion, however, seems to rest on a misunderstanding of the context in which he wrote. Modern theories of the atonement have been developed in order to accommodate ethical objections to penal substitution, and most discussion of the subject since the fifth century has been within the liturgical context of the eucharist.[23] Tertullian, however, saw no objection to penal substitution[24] and had little interest in eucharistic doctrine. The atonement was Christ's great work of justification by which the possibility of restored communion between God and man was opened up. This communion was not primarily a participation in the divine life after the manner of Irenaeus, however.[25] It is difficult to explain the subtle difference between the two men without doing one or the other an injustice, but in general terms, Irenaeus envisaged an essentially mystical communion with God, whereas Tertullian was more concerned with the practical everyday implications of Christian obedience. For this reason his concept of sanctification laid much greater stress on moral activity in the present life and said little which might suggest the beatific vision.

The difference of approach between Irenaeus and Tertullian cannot be explained by temperamental or cultural factors only. However much Tertullian may have been influenced by a Roman sense of legalism, it remains true that the fundamental cause of the divergence between them lay in their different conceptions of sin and evil. Irenaeus thought that ultimately human sin was due to finitude, whereas Tertullian, though he accepted the logical consequences of finitude, attributed responsibility for actual sin to the disobedience of the will. It was this difference which in the long term led to the development of separate theological traditions in East and West. Their mutual incompatibility did not become apparent until the debate over the procession of the Holy Spirit, when the inability to find a common formula led to schism.[26]

This may seem to be an extravagant claim to make for the effects of the difference between Irenaeus and Tertullian over the nature of sin, but in fact later developments were the logical outworking of these two divergent principles. If the cause of sin was different, it was only to be expected that redemption and sanctification would also be understood differently. Irenaeus, with his understanding of sin as the natural result of man's creaturehood, was obviously preoccupied with the need to overcome this ontological disability. As a result he placed much greater emphasis on the incarnation as the prototype of the transcendent life in which the creaturely finitude of man was transformed by grace into the perfection of the divine life. This was the vision of man's destiny which was later to be termed *theōsis* (deification), by which man was able to transcend the present limitations of his finitude and participate directly in the life of God.[27]

In this scheme it was only natural that a trinitarian doctrine should insist that the Father alone was the fountainhead of Deity. Christ as mediator had come to reveal the Father to man, so that he might participate in the Father's life even as the Son did. It was the work of the Holy Spirit to apply the life and example of Christ to the individual, to form Christ, the perfect image and likeness of God, in every believer. This was not an end in itself, but the means of access to the Father in whose life the Christian was called to participate. It was therefore necessary to insist that the Holy Spirit proceeded from the Father alone and that the Son had manifested him from all eternity, without himself being a source of his divinity.[28]

Tertullian, however, had no room in his theology for Irenaeus' latent concept of deification. He too was concerned with the ontological significance of evil, but unlike Irenaeus he perceived clearly that this could not be attributed, even indirectly, to the mere fact of human finitude. A good creator could only bring forth a good creation in which each substance, though certainly inferior, was nevertheless perfect in its own nature. The existence of evil was therefore rooted exclusively in the act of rebellion of the creature against the will of the Creator. For this reason it was impossible to excuse the sinfulness of man by an appeal to the inherent deficiency of his finitude. Man was not obliged to rebel but had chosen to do so of his own free will and was therefore responsible for his action. Tertullian certainly agreed with Irenaeus that Jesus Christ, the incarnate Son of God, was the perfect manifestation of divine humanity, but he interpreted this in terms of obedience rather than essence, at least as far as its wider application to mankind as a whole was concerned. Ontologically speaking Tertullian believed that the divinity of Jesus was unique in kind as well as in degree, and that his incarnation had a definite purpose, which was the atonement.

The barrier of sin between God and man was broken down in Christ not by the fact of his transcendent being in which no man could truly share, but by his perfect sacrifice *in the flesh*, by which he paid the price of human sin (*Adv. Marc* iii.8.4–6). It was the work of the Holy Spirit to make this act of redemption effective in the life of the Christian, so that he might live the life of the incarnate Son of God *as an end in*

itself. The goal of the regenerate believer was not the transcendence of human finitude but the fulfilment of it along the lines
of the incarnation of Jesus Christ the Second Adam. To put it
another way, where Irenaeus and the later Eastern tradition
emphasised participation in the life of the Father through the
Son by the Holy Spirit, Tertullian, and after him the West,
spoke of obedience to the Father in the Son through the Holy
Spirit. The goal of the Christian life was not a mystical
participation in the ineffable essence of God the Father, but
rather the imitation of the Son who had made him known to
men. It was the work of the Holy Spirit, therefore, to reveal
the will of the Father in the obedience of the Son and to
emphasise the complete harmony and equality between them.
Western theologians could not admit that the imitation of the
Son was a lesser grace than participation in the life of the
Father, which in any case they regarded as the same thing. It
was for this reason that as time went on they felt increasingly
bound to uphold a double procession of the Spirit, to avoid
compromising the full ontological deity of the Son.

We may be grateful to Tertullian for having discovered a
more biblical view of the nature of sin than Irenaeus' thinly
disguised Platonism, and for having developed in the light of
his appreciation of the original goodness of finite creatures, a
concept of immanent holiness (sanctification) as opposed to the
transcendent holiness (deification) of the Eastern tradition. But
although we can accept Tertullian's basic principle without
demur, we must also recognise that its subsequent application
in his theology followed other principles which were less biblical,
and which eventually compromised the value of this particular
insight. The fundamental difficulty lay in Tertullian's definition
of immanence. For him the work of Christ on the cross was
archetypal, but it had a purely objective character. The
individual who wished to appropriate Christ's redemptive work
to himself had first to confess Christ as his saviour and repent
of his sins. Bare faith was not enough, however. As an act of
the mind and will, faith was the response of the soul only. True
salvation required the participation of the flesh as well, a fact
which Christ himself had provided for in the physical rite of
baptism.

Baptism was the sacrament in which the Holy Spirit acted

through an earthly substance to reverse the effects of human sin. It was both the mirror of the incarnation and the exact counterpart in reverse of the process by which human sinfulness had manifested itself. Like the human body, the sacrament of baptism was a union of two substances, one divine and one earthly, and it was this exact correspondence to the body which made it efficacious in the removal of sin. In his *De baptism* Tertullian put as much emphasis on the need for water in administration as he did on the inclusion of the flesh in redemption, and many commentators have interpreted this as the refutation of a spiritualising 'gnosticism', which viewed the use of water in baptism as superfluous and unworthy of God Tertullian certainly did encounter objections of this kind though their supposedly 'gnostic' origins remain mysterious but it seems likely that the main factor in his mind was the logical connection between water and the flesh, both of which were earthly substances.

The special correspondence between water and the flesh gave it another great importance as well. As a symbol of cleansing water was obviously extremely familiar, and Tertullian found no difficulty in appealing to Scripture in support of its use But because sin had first penetrated to the soul by way of the flesh, it was logically necessary, in a recaptulative scheme of redemption, for it to be purified in preparation for the Spirit' entry into the soul. An earthly substance could be purified only by one of a like nature, and it was this which gave water its special significance. Tertullian was at great pains to explain the importance of the visible sign and the completeness of its correspondence to the work of the Spirit in the soul (*De resur mort.* 8).

The intimacy of the connection must not obscure the fact that the descent of the Spirit on the soul was not identical with the administration of water (*De bapt.* 6.1). John had baptised with water, but although his baptism 'unto repentance was valid as far as it went, it lacked the fullness of true Christian baptism (ibid., 12). Christian converts who had received John's baptism were consecrated by the laying on of hands, which symbolised the descent of the Spirit. Later candidates for baptism were anointed with oil for the same reason (ibid., 7). It thus appears that the baptism of John was incomplete but not heretical; indeed it was fully acceptable in so far as the administration of water was concerned. There was no magical or quasi-magical importance attached to the rite itself, but only the assurance of grace to accompany its right reception by faith (ibid., 18.6).

The most difficult problem which Tertullian faced over the administration of baptism was undoubtedly the danger of unworthy reception. Although he believed that faith was an essential part of the sacrament's efficacy, it did not follow that where faith was lacking the rite of baptism was no more than an empty ritual. On the contrary, a baptised person who continued in sin was guilty of spurning the grace of God – so much so that his apostasy could be atoned for only by the shedding of his own blood in imitation of Christ (ibid., 16). It is in the light of this that we must understand his reluctance to baptise infants. A child with no knowledge of the importance of the sacrament could easily sin in later life, thereby cancelling the effects of his baptism without ever having been given a fair chance to make a serious commitment to a life of holiness (ibid., 18.4–5). In this instance it was the fear of post-baptismal sin, rather than any question of infant faith or lack of it, which determined Tertullian's attitude.

Yet in the final analysis it was not baptism but the subsequent perseverance of the saints which was the subject closest to Tertullian's heart. It was after baptism in fact, not before it, that the real struggle between the Spirit and the lusts of the flesh set in (*De mono.* 1.3; *De resurr. mort.* 10.3). For baptism was a rite of purification which did no more than restore the flesh and the soul to their natural state. As far as the soul was concerned that was enough; its divine origin was sufficient to ensure its ultimate redemption. But the flesh was still an earthly substance with all the weakness which had caused Adam to sin in the first place. The presence of so fragile a perfection in a fallen world created a tension, the strain of which can only be imagined. For not only was it possible to lose for ever the redeeming virtue of Christ's passion; without constant vigilance and discipline such an eventuality was only too probable. To prevent this from happening, Tertullian was obliged to develop an increasingly rigid asceticism, which in spirit departed more and more from New Testament principles. He continued to search the Scriptures of course, but as time went on he used them increasingly for support rather than for illumination. How this happened is the theme of the last two chapters of this book, and it is to this that we now turn.

CHAPTER FOUR

THE PATTERN OF AUTHORITY

There is no doubt that spiritual discipline was the keystone of Tertullian's scheme of sanctification. This may seem straight-forward enough to us, who have inherited a long tradition of orderly devotion, but in the Roman world of the second century such a concept was bound to meet with certain difficulties in the way of practical application. No one who has studied ancient history can fail to appreciate the administrative genius which enabled Rome to conquer and to hold her Mediterranean empire, but this efficiency in matters of secular organisation did not as a rule extend into the religious sphere. About the only act of worship which the imperial authorities required or made any attempt to regulate was the worship of the emperor's genius. Beyond that, a great variety of religious activity was tolerated, although attempts were sometimes made to suppress particular rites, especially if they offended public decency.

This is not to say that Roman religion was a lax affair, or that it completely failed to command the allegiance of the masses. There is a good deal to suggest that even the cultured intelligentsia preserved a living interest in cultic matters, and religious officials, especially the Vestal Virgins, were widely respected. The difficulty was that Roman religion was bound up with the semi-tribal apparatus of the city-state, and its decay was part of the general breakdown of republican institutions. Various emperors tried to arrest the decline, but even they hardly got further than introducing a form of emperor-worship. This new cult served an obvious political purpose, but in spirit it was essentially alien to the Roman mind. Emperors were chosen and deposed by the senate and people of Rome (which in practice usually meant the army), and there was no concept of divine right. An elected divinity was not likely to be accorded much respect, especially as it was obvious that he would soon have a successor who might well choose to execrate his memory. In this respect, the Roman Empire was not dissimilar from modern totalitarian countries like the Soviet Union.

Because they lacked any truly credible authority, the strict moral precepts of Roman religion were generally defenceless against the inroads of foreign fertility cults, whose obscene practices are recorded with disgust by contemporary historians. When Christianity appeared at Rome, it was to encounter a traditional paganism which had been plunged into moral, spiritual and cultic chaos. It soon became apparent, however, that the new faith was of a different order altogether. The ethical precepts of Christianity were not necessarily stricter than those of paganism, but – and this is a matter of the most crucial importance – they came backed by the authority of a written Revelation from an Omnipotent Creator and Redeemer, a fact which gave them universal significance and eternal validity.

When educated Romans like Tertullian became Christians, they were not unnaturally struck by this aspect of their new faith. In the Greek world the universality of Christianity was assimilated to the philosophical concept of a divinely ordered kosmos, in which the rich diversity of human culture and experience could find its fulfilment and purpose. Romans, however, tended to think in more severely practical terms. 'Spiritual unity' had little meaning for them apart from its visible manifestation. Moreover, if Christianity embraced the whole of life, then there could be virtually no adiaphora, or elements which were not governed by divine regulation.

Thus we can understand why Tertullian devoted an entire treatise to the seemingly trivial question of the veiling of virgins. We may gather from his remarks that most Christians had no very strong feelings on the matter, and preferred not to bother. Scripture enjoined married women to cover their heads in church to indicate their subjection to their husbands, but unmarried girls were not mentioned, and customs apparently varied from place to place. Such laxity Tertullian could not tolerate. He argued from the ambivalence of the Greek word gynē (woman, wife) that women could not be divided into two classes, the married and the unmarried, and this meant that a discipline laid down for women with husbands should naturally extend to the unmarried and widowed as well.[1] To the objection that some obscure tribes had other notions of modesty, and did not require veiling, Tertullian blandly replied that this was the effect of original sin, tolerated to be sure by divine grace until the final revelation of the truth, but never approved of, and on no account to be imitated by others (*De vir. vel.* 2.1).

It is tempting to ascribe such rigorism to his temperament, or to the influence of Montanism, but the problem is not so simple. Rigidity to the point of enforced uniformity of practice, as well as belief, has always been a feature of the Western Church. Even today there is a ready tendency to confuse doctrinal orthodoxy with outward conformity in behaviour, and Tertullian's leanings in this direction are not as eccentric as they might appear. To discover the hidden motivations behind his censure, therefore, we must lay aside superficial theories about his personality and examine more closely the assumptions on which his theological system was built.

THE REGULA

There can be no doubt that a Roman sense of legalism was fundamental to Tertullian's way of thinking. Even in his analysis of the practice of baptism, for instance, we can see the judicial mind at work. Why should such a rite exist at all? Tertullian explains that it was because Jesus himself, shortly before his ascension, had promulgated a law on the subject, and had even imposed a form for administering the rite, which Tertullian actually called the *lex tingendi* (*De bapt.* 13.3). Of course, if the sacrament of Christian initiation was governed by a legal ordinance, we may be certain that the life of the newly initiated believer would not escape similar regulation.

It was an unfortunate (though characteristic) tendency of Adolf Harnack to seize on a valuable insight – in this case, Tertullian's legalism – and then misapply it in his research. Thus a great deal of scholarly effort has been expended in debate over whether or not the terms *persona* and *substantia*, as Tertullian used them of the Trinity, were derived from legal usage, and even whether the Carthaginian theologian could be identified with the rather obscure jurist of the same name. Both these suggestions have now been rightly rejected,[2] but the debates over them have undoubtedly obscured the very real influence which Roman legal thought, then in its greatest flowering, had on Tertullian's intellectual formation.

Of course this influence must not be exaggerated or misunderstood. Tertullian did not adapt Christianity to Roman law, but the reverse. No one could fail to notice how important the idea of law was in the Old Testament, and Tertullian was well aware, as Marcion and others were not, that Christ had come to fulfil the Law, not to destroy it. Even in the new dispensation, the rule of law, no longer written on tablets of stone but on the table of the heart, continued to be normative for the Christian.[3] Indeed, Tertullian believed that the Gospel had given mankind the power at last to fulfil the Law's strict demands. Jesus himself had said that the righteousness of the Christian was to exceed the righteousness of the scribes and Pharisees, which Tertullian regarded as entirely a matter of degree (*De mono.* 7.1).

As far as the text of God's Law was concerned, there could be no real dispute. Scripture was the Law of God, written down in plain language which everyone could understand and obey (*De praescr. haer.* 14.3). Tertullian knew that the Bible was not always equally clear on every point, and that it did not cover everything, but he never allowed either fact to obscure his main thesis. Those who sought refuge in allegory to explain away moral and philosophical difficulties in Scripture met with the same rebuff as those who tried to excuse non-biblical practices on the ground that Scripture said nothing about them. The principles which guided Tertullian's exegesis were simplicity and caution. What Scripture did not explicitly affirm, it implicitly denied (*De mono.* 4.4). Likewise, it was better to obey the clear commands of God than to make them more palatable to sophisticated consciences (*De praescr. haer.* 14.2).

The legal status with which Tertullian invested the Bible may be seen most clearly from the way it was meant to be interpreted and used in the Church. As we have already remarked in our discussion of pre-credal dogmatism, the word which constantly reappears in this connection is the legal term *regula*. Modern research into the history of credal development has made us familiar with the so-called *regula fidei* ('Rule of Faith') which is thought to have been a statement of doctrine in existence at least from the second century, and which probably formed the basis of the creeds as we now have them. Quite what the *regula fidei* was, however, is a matter of dispute. At one extreme are the views of Dom Bernard Capelle, who writes: '... at the risk of being practically inapplicable, the notion of the *regula fidei* presupposes that it was something formulated in unambiguous terms, in an official document handed to the believer ... the hypothesis of a composite and personalized text must be excluded.'[4] Capelle goes on to argue that the *regula fidei* was identical to the baptismal confession, which seems to have become more standardised about this time.

The proposed link between the *regula fidei* and the baptismal confession has been strongly contested by J. M. Restrepo-Jaramillo, who cites three main arguments in support of his case. First, the baptismal confession contained only trinitarian statements, whereas the *regula fidei* extended to every aspect of the revelation; second, the confession had three sections, in line with its trinitarian structure, whereas the *regula* had only two; third, the confession contained articles on the Church and the forgiveness of sins which the *regula* omitted.[5] Although the first and the third of these objections would appear to contradict each other, Restrepo-Jaramillo's argument points in the right direction, and its main lines were incorporated by J. N. D. Kelly in his *Early Christian Creeds* (p. 82). It is now widely accepted that the baptismal confession, though in many respects similar to the *regula fidei*, cannot be identified with it.

It would seem that this conclusion is shared also, at least tacitly, by Vincent Morel. His view is more flexible than Capelle's, and he places much less weight on verbal agreements. Morel recognises that Tertullian was inconsistent in his formulation of the *regula fidei*, but claims that a general pattern is discernible. The decisive difference between the *regula* and the baptismal confession was the former's omission of the clauses dealing with the Church and the forgiveness of sins. To Capelle's suggestion that Tertullian may have left them out by accident, Morel replies:

A casual omission of these two truths is, on the other hand, quite improbable, since the omission is consistent and the concern of the moment, which always left a strong imprint on Tertullian's formulations of the rule, would have required a mention of them, in the *De praescriptione haereticorum* as well as in the *De virginibus velandis*. Tertullian is trying to be exhaustive, and intends to determine in an absolute way, what Christians might discuss, and what in Christianity is or is not susceptible to development or reform. Thus there is no reason, in our opinion, to speak of an omission, either by chance or by design, and the conclusion that Tertullian, even as a Catholic, did not consider the doctrines of the constitution of the Church and of the forgiveness of sins as part of the rule of faith, forces itself upon us.[6]

But though Morel is prepared to allow for greater latitude than Capelle, fundamentally he also believes that the *regula fidei* was a definite formula, not perhaps fixed in the strict sense, but none the less clear in outline. To prove his point, he cites the text of the *regula* as it occurs in *De praescriptione haereticorum* and in *De virginibus velandis*. At first sight his case seems plausible enough, but on closer examination it will be seen that the differences between the two 'complete' formulae are such as to make his entire thesis untenable. To prove our point we quote them here in parallel form:

De vir. vel. 1.3	*De praescr. haer.* 13.1–5
Regula quidem fidei una omnino est sola immobilis et irreformabilis, credendi scilicet	*Regula est autem fidei ut iam hinc quid defendamus profiteamur, illa scilicet qua creditur.*
in unicum Deum omnipotentem mundi conditorem	*Unum omnino Deum esse nec aliud praeter mundi conditorem qui universa de nihilo produxerit per verbum suum.*
et filium eius Jesum Christum natum ex virgine Maria	*Id verbum filium eius appellatum in nomine Dei varie visum patriarchis in prophetis semper auditum, postremo delatum e spiritu patris Dei et virtute in virginem Mariam, carnem factum in utero eius et ex ea natum egiss Jesum Christum.*

Exinde praedicasse novam legem et novam promissionem regni cae-lorum, virtutes fecisse.

cruci fixum sub Pontio Pilato	*cruci fixum*
tertia die resuscitatum a mortuis	*tertia die resurrexisse*
receptum in caelis, sedentem nunc ad dexteram Patris	*in caelos ereptum sedisse ad dexteram Patris*
	misisse vicarium vim Spiritus Sancti qui credentes agat
venturum iudicare vivos et mortuos per carnis etiam resurrectionem.	*venturum cum claritate ad sumendos sanctos in vitae aeternae et promis-sorum caelestium fructum et ad profanos iudicandos igni perpetuo, facta utriusque partis resuscita-tione cum carnis restitutione.*

A comparison of these two statements reveals that the formula recorded in *De praescriptione* is, generally speaking, much more detailed, except, interestingly enough, in the clauses which deal with the crucifixion and the resurrection. It shows also that the *De virginibus* passage is considerably closer to the Apostles' Creed as we now have it, a fact which is of some interest, since this treatise is usually thought to be of Montanist inspiration. Morel's claim that 'the concern of the moment' influenced the content and wording of the statements may be doubted; what, for instance, did Pontius Pilate have to do with the veiling of virgins? Similarly, Montanist influence on the *De virginibus* can hardly explain the differences, since references to the Holy Spirit and to the teaching of Christ as a *nova lex* are confined to the 'Catholic' *De praescriptione*.[7]

Both passages cover much the same ground, but specific points of contact between them are few. It is clearly to be expected that the Persons of the Trinity should be mentioned in the traditional order, and that the events of Christ's earthly life should be put down in chronological sequence. Beyond that, however, there are not many similarities. Even key words in the theological vocabulary are different – *resuscitatum* instead of

resurrexisse, receptum instead of *ereptum*, for example. In the light
of these discrepancies, not to mention the evident freedom with
which Tertullian expanded his basic theme, it seems impossible
to define the *regula* as a proto-creed. It is true that the creeds
were later composed on models of this kind, but there is no
trace in Tertullian of the sacramental context in which creeds
were mainly used.

The meaning of *regula* in Tertullian is best appreciated, we
believe, by seeing it in the context of his own age. In its
primary sense, *regula* means something straight, a rod or a staff.
From there it came naturally to mean a measuring-rod, and
was used by Cicero to translate the Greek *kanōn*, or standard
measure. In philosophical terminology *kanōn* (*regula*) meant a
standard, or criterion for distinguishing right from wrong, true
from false. It was in this sense that the word entered the
vocabulary of the Greek Apologists, and especially Irenaeus,
who spoke of *ho kanōn tēs alētheias*, the standard or rule of truth,
against which all doctrine must be measured.[8]

There is good evidence that Tertullian borrowed this term
from Irenaeus (cf. *De pud.* 8.12: *regula veritatis*), but his use of it
went some way beyond Irenaeus' rather vague conception.
There is little reason in fact to doubt that Tertullian was
strongly influenced in this by the development which the word
had undergone at the hands of the Roman jurists of the first and
second centuries. As Peter Stein has demonstrated, they took
the word from the Greek grammarians, who used *kanōn* to mean
a rule of syntax, and applied it to Roman law.[9] In the process,
regula developed its hitherto largely descriptive sense to take in
a prescriptive meaning as well. In Stein's words, '*regula* ...
connoted to a Roman of the early principate a normative
proposition which governed all situations which could be sub-
sumed under its *ratio*' (p. 66). As such, a *regula* possessed great
authority in the science of legal interpretation. When the
meaning of a particular statute was unclear or open to different understandings, it was by consulting his *regulae* that a
lawyer or judge could discern the sense intended.

It should be emphasised, of course, that legal *regulae* had no
independent authority; at most they were but résumés of the
law, to which they were subordinate. This is brought out quite
clearly by the jurist Paul, who wrote:

Regula est quae rem quae est breviter enarrat. Non ex regula ius sumatur, sed ex iure quod est regula fiat. Per regulam igitur brevis rerum narratio traditur, et, ut ait Sabinus, quasi causae coniectio est, quae simul cum aliquo vitiata est, perdit officium suum.

A *regula* is that which explains briefly what the matter is. The law must not be deduced from the *regula*, but the *regula* is determined by what the law is. By means of the *regula* therefore, a short summary of things is passed on, and, as Sabinus says, it is like the (official) résumé of a case, which, as soon as it is tampered with, loses its authority.[10]

As long as a *regula* faithfully reflected its original, the jurists of the classical period were not unduly concerned with its precise formulation; only in Byzantine times did this become a matter for strict codification.

When we apply Stein's findings to Tertullian we discover that the latter's use of the word *regula* ties in perfectly with contemporary legal practice. The *regula fidei* was the summary of the *lex* (i.e. Scripture) which could then be used as the fundamental rule in biblical interpretation. However, faith was not the only aspect of scriptural teaching which was ordered by a *regula*; discipline also came under a similar form of control. In fact the phrase *regula disciplinae* is about as frequent, and certainly as important, as the expression *regula fidei* in Tertullian. Moreover, like the *regula fidei*, the *regula disciplinae* had existed from the beginning, long before the appearance of the first heretics (*Adv. Prax.* 2.2).

Tertullian strongly objected to any suggestion that the Apostles had enjoined a relaxation of the role of discipline found in the Old Testament law, as we can see from his remarks on the subject of adultery (*De pud.* 12.2–3):

Non in Apostolis quoque veteris legis forma soluta circa moechiae quanta sit demonstrationem, ne forte lenior existimetur in novitate disciplinarum quam in vetustate. Cum primum intonuit evangelium et vetera concussit, ut de legis retinendae necessitate disceptaretur, primum hanc regulam de auctoritate Spiritus Sancti Apostoli emittunt ad eos qui iam ex nationibus allegi coeperant ...

Do we not recognize the form of the old law with regard to the demonstration of adultery and how serious it is, in the

Apostles also, lest it be thought more trivial in the new (dispensation) than in the old? When the Gospel first sounded forth and shattered the old order, so that it was debated whether or not the law should be retained, this was the first rule which the Apostles, on the authority of the Holy Spirit, sent to those who were beginning to be gathered from among the nations ...

But although faith and discipline were each subject to a *regula*, there were great differences between them. The most important of these was that the rule of faith was fixed for all time. The facts and pattern of redemption were eternal – *veritas semper et antiqua res* – but the rule of discipline was not (*De vir. vel.* 1.2). The variability of the *regula disciplinae* was certainly not arbitrary, as we shall see, though there is no doubt that it did cause Tertullian some embarrassment. Whatever disadvantages there may have been, however, were outweighed by the one supreme advantage which it gave him. For by insisting that spiritual discipline could and did become stricter in the course of time, Tertullian was able to short-circuit those of his opponents who appealed to the *example* of Scripture to govern their conduct (thereby avoiding, so Tertullian would argue, its more rigorous *precepts*). To understand this line of reasoning, and the way in which the rule of discipline operated, we must examine the analysis he gave of the workings of Divine Providence, and in particular his understanding of the dispensations of salvation history.

THE DISPENSATIONS AND DISCIPLINE

Tertullian saw the unfolding of salvation as a historical process in three distinct phases, which corresponded to the Old Testament, the Incarnation of Christ and the Pentecostal reign of the Holy Spirit. Norman Cohn has seen in this teaching a primitive form of the millenarianism developed by the mediaeval mystic Joachim of Fiore, and transmitted through him to a wide variety of popular protest movements in the later Middle Ages.[11] Whether this was so or not, there can be no doubt that Tertullian's dispensational scheme, even if its elements did not originate with him, represented a radical departure from much of what the Church as a whole had previously taught. This was perhaps the chief single reason for the opposition which his disciplinary injunctions encountered in the more sophisticated ecclesiastical circles.

Tertullian was preoccupied with the problem of time. We have already seen how he distinguished between the temporal image and the eternal likeness of God (both of which, of course, were united in Christ) and this carried over into his christology and his trinitarian theology. The problem may be stated briefly as follows. God's will and plan for Adam's race is eternal and immutable. Adam, however, chose to exercise his free will and disobeyed God's decrees. But God was not content to abandon his creation, so he resolved to redeem man by teaching him to obey the Divine Law. This instruction was given in three historical stages (*dispositiones*), in each of which a different Person of the Trinity took the leading role.[12] In the first of these stages, or dispensations, God revealed the *content* of the Divine Law, which was subsequently interpreted by the Prophets (*De vir. vel.* 1.7). In dealing with the Old Covenant, Tertullian generally followed St Paul, though there is some indication that he played down the Abrahamic origins of Israel's faith and put more emphasis on Moses than was warranted, particularly in the matter of circumcision. It is somewhat strange, for example, that although he speaks of faith without the need for circumcision, and of circumcision being a spiritual as well as a physical act, he never mentions the fact that the sign had originally been given to Abraham because of his faith (*Adv. Marc.* v. 4.8–10).

The first dispensation was that of the Father, and Tertullian was at great pains to point out the logical continuity of the plan of God through the trinitarian dispensations, in opposition especially to the Marcionites, who rejected the Old Testament (ibid., v.4.1). The first dispensation held good until the time of John the Baptist, last of the line of prophets. Did Tertullian teach that there was a precise moment at which the dispensation of the Father became the dispensation of the Son? There is some evidence that he regarded the moment of Christ's baptism as the point at which the change occurred,[13] which, if true, would tie in very well with the great importance which he attached to the rite. On the other hand, he frequently quoted

Luke 16.16 (*lex et prophetae usque ad Iohannem*) without any mention of baptism.[14] It is therefore possible that he regarded the two dispensations as partially overlapping in the time between Christ's baptism and John's death. Such a view would tie in with John's own statements in Scripture (John 3.30), but it may not have commended itself so easily to one as conscious of time as Tertullian was. The answer is probably that, of these alternatives, the former would have appealed most to Tertullian and comes closest to what he actually believed.

For our purposes we may assume that it was the baptism of Christ which marked the beginning of the second dispensation, in which the chief role was played by the Son. In the overall context of the Divine Law, this new revelation of God was of the greatest significance. For Christ was the *supplementum legis et prophetarum* (*Adv. Marc.* iv.2.2), and *nostra lex ampliata atque suppleta* (*De orat.* 22.8). In him the Law of God which during the old dispensation had been hidden in parables and allegories, was made manifest in its fullness (*De resurr. mort.* 19–21). In Christ the sentence of death on sinful Adam was annulled, and eternal life made available to men (*De pud.* 9.6). Tertullian never thought for a moment that Jesus had revealed anything fundamentally new. In keeping with the pattern of recapitulation, the work of Christ was one of revelation in the most literal sense – he had come to unveil the truth which had been present from the start in shadows and types (*Adv. Marc.* v.11.5–7). The life and death of Jesus, therefore, formed an extended commentary on, and fulfilment of, the divinely appointed Law.

It was in the final element of his dispensational scheme, however, that Tertullian was at his most original, and where his views, often in remarkably unmodified form, are still capable of provoking controversy.[15] The prominence which Tertullian gave to the reign of the Paraclete is not surprising when we consider that it was, after all, the age in which he and his contemporaries were living. But it was also the period for which there was the least amount of divine instruction available. The prophets of Israel had been around to interpret the first dispensation as need arose, and the Apostles had explained the second, but who was there to carry on this work in the third? In theory, the answer seemed obvious enough. The prophet Joel had predicted that in the last days God would pour out his Spirit on all flesh, and this promise had been remembered and repeated on the Day of Pentecost (ibid., v.8.6). On the nature of these spiritual gifts, both Isaiah the prophet and St Paul the Apostle were in complete agreement, a point which Tertullian raised in his attack on Marcion (ibid., v.8.8.).

The theory, so it seemed, was clear enough. But where were these new prophets who were supposed to guide the Church? Montanus was clearly one, and even at Carthage there were occasional examples of prophetic ecstasy.[16] But these were the exceptions which only served to confirm the rule – the new spiritual life was not evident in the majority of cases. In recognising this, Tertullian both conformed to and sharply dissented from the so-called 'gnostic' picture of the Church. He agreed with the Valentinians and others that there were two kinds of Christian – the *spiritalis* and the *psychicus*, but differed radically from them as to the reasons why this was so. In the 'gnostic' scheme, the *psychici* were intellectually deficient, since they had no knowledge of those higher spiritual realities, which went under the name of the Aeon, the Pleroma and the Nous. Tertullian rejected all this as mythological nonsense, which is hardly surprising, given his conception of revelation as the unveiling of the Divine Law. Knowledge was not the problem, since everything there was to know had already been revealed in Christ. The real difficulty lay deeper, at the level of experience.

In Tertullian's scheme, the transition from the second to the third dispensation was neither as neat nor as sudden as the switch from the first to the second. Instead of being instantaneous, it occurred in two steps over a ten-day period. The first of these, of course, was the Ascension, which represented not only the culmination of the earthly work of Christ, but even more important, the beginning of a new relationship between man and God. For it was in ascending that 'he led captivity captive, and *gave gifts to men*' (ibid., v.8.5). These gifts materialised ten days afterwards at Pentecost, when the Holy Spirit descended on the disciples. The significance of this event was enormous. The Spirit brought no new knowledge (*De mono.* 3.9), but he did bring something equally important – the power to put the teaching and example of Christ into practice. In the

third dispensation, the Law-fulfilling life of the one Man was
to become the standard for all, and it was the task of the
Paraclete to make this feasible (ibid., 4.1). The dividing line
between spiritual and unspiritual Christians was not one of
knowledge, therefore, but of sanctification.

Tertullian's use of the term *Paracletus* to qualify the Holy
Spirit is significant for the light it sheds on the unity of the
dispensations. Its importance as a badge of Montanism has
been greatly exaggerated, with the unfortunate result that its
real significance has been obscured. For the word *Paracletus*,
taken as it is from Jesus' promise to his disciples that he would
not leave them bereft,[17] emphasised as nothing else could do
the close link between the work of the Holy Spirit and the
Person of Christ. The task of the Paraclete was to conform men
to Christ so that they could follow his holy example more closely.
In them, he would translate into reality the full implications
of the Incarnation. The Law which had been revealed to Moses
and fulfilled in Christ would now be written on the heart of
every *spiritalis* by the Divine Comforter himself.

Tertullian's dispensationalism, important though it was,
should not be confused with millenarianism in the usual sense.
There is no doubt that he believed that Christians were living
in the last days, but this belief was always tempered with
practical considerations which were far more important in his
teaching. He took the Apocalypse seriously, of course, and
believed it more or less literally, but it is significant that he
confined himself to repeating a catalogue of the expected events
and did not indulge in speculation about the Beast and so on
(cf. e.g., *De resurr. mort.* 27.1). Considering that millenarianism
was at this time widely accepted in the Church, even by people
as hard-headed as Irenaeus, and that Tertullian sympathised
publicly with the Montanists, who were millenarians of the
first order, this is perhaps somewhat surprising. But it is less so
if we consider what his main purpose was in developing his
dispensational ideas in the first place.

Tertullian needed dispensationalism not for supernatural
reasons, but in order to provide a solid theological basis on
which to build his disciplinary structure. This is clear from the
way in which he handled moral precepts and their application.
It was obvious, for instance, that for some reason a different

standard was applied to adulterers in the New Testament from that which had obtained under the Mosaic Law. On the one hand Jesus himself had altered the Law's provisions (or so it seemed), and perhaps made possible further modifications later on, by transferring the power of binding and loosing to his disciples. But at the same time, Scripture clearly stated that the gospel was everlasting and unchanging. How could these two apparently contradictory statements be reconciled?

Tertullian's solution of this dilemma was ingenious. As he explained it, both faith and discipline existed in principle from the beginning, though in both cases the revelation of the details proceeded by stages. The discipline of the Old Testament, like the faith of the Israelites, was incomplete. Because of this God excused some of the people's failings, by the grace which Tertullian called his *indulgentia*, until the fullness of the revelation should come (*De exhort. cast.* 3.2). The advent of Christ brought an end to this period of tolerance, but God's *indulgentia* was not immediately withdrawn. Even after Pentecost the Apostles continued to allow remarriage, for instance, even though it was against the principles of the creation settlement (*De pud.* 20.1–4). The reason for this, however, was only that since sinful human beings could not change their habits overnight, the Apostles had been instructed to proceed leniently and by stages with the application of the full weight of the discipline revealed in Christ. This period of extended indulgence had lasted 160 years, but now, Tertullian claimed, it was to be wound up (*De mono.* 3.8). How and why was this?

It was at this point that Tertullian's line of reasoning began to diverge seriously from New Testament principles. The Apostles had taught that the last days had arrived, and their decisions, in matters of discipline as well as of faith, were regarded as final. But Tertullian wished to impose a stricter moral régime than the one the Apostles had tolerated. He therefore had to show that the moral behaviour of the New Testament Church, including the Apostles' advice, was inferior to the precepts which these same Apostles had laid down as normative. He also had to show that the Holy Spirit had since filled the gap left in Scripture with a completed teaching of his own.

This extraordinary course was not as difficult as it might

appear, however. The main lines of the New Testament teaching on marriage had been set out by St Paul in his letters to the Corinthians, but it was on this subject that he had shown the greatest degree of hesitation. He had even acknowledged that he had no direct command from God, but only the mind of the Spirit to guide him (*De exhort. cast.* 4.4; *De cor.* 4.6; *De pud.* 16.21). For Tertullian this was literally a godsend. If the Apostle himself had no specific instructions, then it was obvious that the advice which he gave was not in the same category as his other pronouncements. This did not mean that it carried no weight at all, of course, but rather that its authority was of a special nature. St Paul had spoken on the strength of the Holy Spirit given to him. But clearly he was not the only one to whom the Spirit had been given, and if his views on the marriage question were so uncertain, was it not likely that the Spirit would later provide more detailed instructions through some other spokesman? This was what Tertullian claimed had happened in the prophecies of the Montanists. Their exhortations to chastity and holy living were the final element which completed the divine scheme of sanctification (*De mono.* 3.8).

The particular role of Montanus and his followers in this scheme, however, needs to be treated with some caution. For one thing, Montanus began to prophesy about the year 171, or only 140 years after Pentecost. Since Tertullian says 160 years, he must have been speaking more of his own time than of the previous generation, to which the original Montanists belonged. Then too, the Montanist emphasis on the Paraclete and the descent of the New Jerusalem would suggest that Montanus was heavily influenced by a Johannine outlook, while Tertullian's thought is more Pauline. What place then did Tertullian assign to Montanus? Probably he regarded him and his immediate followers as fulfilling a task analogous to that of John the Baptist, who announced the coming of a Kingdom but was not himself part of it. Both John and Montanus were prophets outside the main tradition, and both heralded the impending arrival of a new order. Like John, Montanus had also been rejected by the religious leaders of the day and his message had gone unheeded. But Tertullian took him seriously, and regarded the New Prophecy as the authentic sign of the approaching end. The conclusion was inescapable – the strictest possible moral discipline must be enforced without delay, so as to be ready for the Second Coming of Christ and the final judgment.

SCRIPTURA, NATURA, DISCIPLINA

The importance of the dispensations for the development of Tertullian's pattern of discipline was reinforced by a wider system of authority involving the universal principles of Scripture and nature. The fullest explanation of their relationship is given in the following passage from *De virginibus velandis* 16.1–2:

> *In his consistit defensio nostrae opinionis secundum Scripturam, secundum naturam, secundum disciplinam. Scriptura legem condit, natura contestatur, disciplina exigit. Cul ex his consuetudo opinionis prodest, vel qui diversae sententiae color? Dei est Scriptura, Dei est natura Dei est disciplina. Quicquid contrarium est istis, Dei non est. Si Scriptura incerta est, natura manifesta est, et de eius testimonio Scriptura incerta non potest esse. Si de natura dubitatur, disciplina quid magis Deo ratum sit ostendit. Nihil est illi carius humilitate, nihil acceptius modestia, nihil operosius gloria et studio hominibus placendi. Illud itaque sit tibi et Scriptura et natura et disciplina quod ratum Deo invereris, sicut iuberis omnia examinare et meliora quaeque sectari* (1 Thess. 5.21).

The defence of our opinion is as follows, according to Scripture, nature and discipline. Scripture establishes the law, nature testifies to it and discipline demands it. Which of these is the primary authority, or what element of diversity is there between them? Scripture is of God, nature is of God, discipline is of God. Whatever goes against these is not of God. If Scripture is uncertain, nature is clear, and from its witness Scripture cannot be uncertain. If nature is unclear, discipline shows what God prefers. Nothing is dearer to him than humility, nothing more welcome than modesty, nothing more burdensome than pride and a desire to please men. Therefore let it be a rule for you, that you will find God's will in Scripture, nature and discipline, as you have been commanded to *examine all things and choose whatever is best* (1 Thess. 5.21).

The key concepts in this passage are contained in the trilogy *Scriptura, natura, disciplina.* At first sight it might appear as if Tertullian accorded equal weight to all three, but a closer inspection will show that this is not the case. The relationship between them is perhaps best compared to that between the Persons of the Trinity. Nor is this likely to have been an accident. Although Tertullian nowhere explained his choice of terms, it is possible that he was guided mainly by trinitarian considerations. Scripture, after all, was given by God the Father, nature was redeemed in Christ, and discipline was applied in the Church through the ministry of the Holy Spirit. The parallel cannot be pressed too far, of course, but the analogy is there none the less. Certainly Scripture is given a pride of place not unlike that accorded to the Father (cf. *Adv. Marc.* iii.20.1). The relation of the Three Persons to the Law is also markedly similar. The law was established by God the Father, its truth witnessed to by the Son, and its provisions enforced by the Holy Spirit.

In Tertullian's trilogy there can be no doubt that a very definite primacy was accorded to Scripture, which alone established the Law. Nature and discipline might clarify it, but only the written text carried the seal of ultimate authority. The Christian who sought to know God's will must begin with the Bible; only when it was unclear could he turn to nature and discipline. Not that Scripture was ever truly unclear, of course – uncertainties of interpretation were due to the inability of men to understand divine truth, not to mistakes on God's part (*De resurr. mort.* 21.2).

As for nature, it is true that Tertullian allowed a secondary appeal to it to clarify obscurities in the Bible, but great care must be taken to understand just exactly what he meant by this term. Nature to him was not the *physis* of Aristotle, still less the *natura* of Thomas Aquinas. Nature was the created state before Adam's corruption by original sin. It is essential to realise that for Tertullian fallen man as we know him was not natural but *unnatural*, in direct contrast to the usual modern usage. His famous remark that the soul was *naturaliter christiana* (*Apol.* 17.6) must be understood in this light.[18] Tertullian was speaking about the created, perfect soul, not the corrupt unregenerate substance actually present in men. It is therefore quite wrong to suppose, as some have done, that Tertullian ever imagined that the 'natural' man (in the Thomist sense) could attain to a knowledge of God independent of revelation. It is true that when Tertullian spoke of man in his actual fallen state, he did use the term *natura* to describe it, but never without qualification, as we have already seen. Like God, the devil too was capable of giving man a nature, although in this case it was but a corruption and a counterfeit of the divine gift.

It is when we come to the third element of the trilogy, however, that we meet the most serious difficulties. We have already seen how the distinction between a principle and its application allowed Tertullian to talk of a *nova disciplina* while at the same time denying accusations that he was introducing this very thing. This was possible because in principle discipline was an unchanging factor in the life of the Church. It had always existed, always been necessary as a defence against sin, and always been mandatory in the pursuit of holiness (*De vir. vel.* 1; *De mono.* 1). In practice, however, discipline, at least as it was applied in the Church, was a potentially variable series of rules and regulations. On the other hand the changes in question were not arbitrary, but based on Scripture and governed by its *ratio* (*De exhort. cast.* 6.2).

The scriptural foundation for discipline and especially the dependence of *ratio* on the written law must be emphasised in view of the fact that many scholars, particularly among Roman Catholics, have tried to find an authority for discipline in unwritten traditions, presumably in an attempt to trace post-Tridentine dogma back to the Apostles themselves. The effects of this approach may be seen in the following from Morel (op. cit., p. 264):

> ...in the development of *disciplina*, the author accords primary importance to *ratio*, i.e. to the rational basis of traditions and extra-Scriptural practices. In this perspective it is natural for a human institution which has shown itself conformable to reason and useful for the good of souls (the hierarchical organization of the Church) to be one day confirmed by the Paraclete and raised from the human institution it was to the rank of a divine one.[19]

This extraordinary statement Morel supports from two

passages, neither of which has the slightest bearing on 'the hierarchical organization of the Church'. The first of these (*De cor.* 4.5) reads as follows:

Porro si ratione lex constat, lex erit omne iam quod ratione constiterit a quocunque productum. An non putas omni fideli licere concipere et constituere, dumtaxat quod Deo congruat, quod disciplinae conducat, quod saluti proficiat . . .

Furthermore if the law stands by *ratio*, everything which stands by *ratio* will be law, whoever (or whatever) it comes from. Or do you not think that it is allowed to every believer to think and formulate, provided that it be what accords with God, leads to discipline and is useful to salvation . . .

This passage is quoted to show that Tertullian regarded *ratio* as an authority superior to law, but it is extremely doubtful whether this is really what is meant here. It is certainly true that he says that the law is determined by *ratio*, but it is important to notice how this was decided in practice. *Lex* in this context does not refer to a text, but to *ad hoc* regulations for which no written provision has been made. This wider meaning is made explicit in the second clause, where *carte blanche* is given to establish further practices as law without recourse to specific legislation. At the same time, however, this process is not arbitrary, nor is it grounded in autonomous human reason. It is not what the Christian deems to be rational which has the force of law, but what accords with the data already known by revelation. Admittedly, Tertullian does not say so explicitly, but since he frequently insists that God and the plan of salvation can be known only by revelation, and also that this revelation exists in written form (*Scriptura*), it seems plain that we are to understand this passage as confirming the primacy of Scripture over *ratio*.

This supposition is confirmed by Morel's second quotation, this time from *De ieiunio* 10.5:

Eorum quae ex traditione observantur tanto magis dignam rationem adferre debemus quanto carent scripturae auctoritate donec aliquo caelesti charismate aut confirmentur aut corrigantur.

As for these things which are observed on account of tradition, we must produce a worthy *ratio*, all the more in that they lack Scriptural authority, until such time as they are either confirmed or altered by some heavenly *charisma*.

Morel believes that this strengthens his case for the independence of *ratio* as a source of authority, but it is difficult to see how this follows from the evidence he cites. It is precisely the lack of scriptural authority which highlights the need for *ratio* in the first place, and even then the practices established in this manner remain subject to modification by some heavenly *charisma*. Tertullian is tantalisingly vague about what this might be, but it would certainly have included prophecy, and experience suggested that prophetic utterances would soon find their way into writing and be added to the existing body of Scripture. Indeed, it seems quite likely that Tertullian has in mind a process similar to the one which produced the New Testament, in which traditional Jewish observances are substantially modified on precisely this basis.

As for Christian discipline, it might be derived from unwritten conventions, but the validity of these was still dependent on their conformity to the *ratio* of Scripture. To quote Tertullian (*De cor.* 4.1):

Harum et aliarum eiusmodi disciplinarum si legem expostules Scripturam nullam leges. Tradition tibi praetendetur auctrix et consuetudo confirmatrix et fides observatrix. Rationem traditioni et consuetudini et fidei patrocinaturam aut ipse perspicies aut ab aliquo qui perspixerit disces.

As for these and other like disciplines, if you demand a law (legal basis) you will find no Scriptural warrant (for them). Tradition is claimed to be the author, custom the sanctioner and faith the observer. The *ratio* which will support the tradition, the custom and the faith – this you may discern for yourself or else learn from someone who has discerned it.

It will be noted that Tertullian does not say *traditio est auctrix* but only *traditio praetendetur auctrix*, a hint that a given practice's origin in tradition was more seeming than real. This is important in view of the fact that it has sometimes been suggested that Tertullian conceived of tradition as an authority distinct from, and even superior to, Scripture.[20] This view, however,

seems to derive from a misunderstanding of the word *ratio*
Fontaine, for example, identifies it with the Stoic concept o
divine harmony, and regards it as the common link betweer
Scripture and tradition, which are otherwise independen
sources of authority. Thus *disciplina* might be derived from
either in the first instance, though ultimately it depended or
ratio.[21] Morel is less explicit, but he too regards *ratio* as funda
mental. The mistake which both Fontaine and Morel hav‹
made, however, is that they have equated *ratio* with 'reason' ir
the philosophical sense, whereas Tertullian used the word in it
legal meaning, which is not the same at all. What *ratio* mean
to a jurist has been explained by Jacques Ellul as follows:

> *Ius est ars aequi et boni*, i.e. the art of finding the mos
> equitable and effective momentary application of a giver
> notion common to all men. This application is made accord
> ing to a precise and established mode of reasoning which th‹
> Roman jurists call *ratio* (which does not mean 'reason'). Thi
> natural law includes institutions like the family and property
> and rules such as the prohibition against stealing or killing
> It is not justice itself. Justice appears as a sort of doubl
> relationship: on the one hand, relationship between natura
> law and the given circumstances in which it is to take form
> and, on the other, relationship between the positive law an‹
> the action of a particular individual.[22]

In Ellul's definition we can discern the legal process by whicl
Tertullian interpreted the Scriptures for the needs of th
Christian community at Carthage. Scripture itself was the law
common to all Christians and accepted by them as authorita
tive. The application of biblical principles was governed b·
traditio (precedent), *consuetudo* (practice) and *fides* (consent)
Operating together, these three factors were the *ratio* by whicl
the written law was administered. This *ratio* was not an inde·
pendent authority, but merely a procedure, by which Scriptur‹
was shown to speak in particular circumstances.[23]

But if Tertullian's use of *ratio* cannot be traced to a philo
sophical source, the same cannot be said for the triadic formul‹
Scriptura, natura, disciplina, the origins of which go back to th‹
pre-Socratic philosophers. Even when we allow for the fact tha
it was a common habit of the Ancients to divide everything

into three parts, there is unmistakable evidence that a combination remarkably like this one enjoyed considerable popularity over a long period. Although different writers, including Tertullian, adjusted the triad to suit their own purposes, there is solid evidence that a definite tradition, well represented in the didactic philosophy of all periods, took hold and was generally accepted from a very early date.

The idea of a triadic formula may well have originated with Protagoras, as an offshoot of his interest in numerology. In Plato's dialogue he is quoted as saying: *ex epimeleias kai askēseōs kai didachēs* (*Prot.* 323d), and there is a well-known fragment which supports this.[24] Other evidence may be found in Democritus,[25] but it is Plato who first used the three-point formula as we know it. Aside from the quotation already given, there is a passage in the *Laws* which reads: *ethesi kai epainois kai logois* (ii. 663d) and a sentence in the *Meno* which says: *Echeis moi eipein, Ō Sōkrates, ara didakton hē aretē ē ou didakton all' askēton, ē oute askēton oute mathēton, alla physei paragignetai tois anthrōpois . . .* The last of these shows perhaps most clearly the basis on which the later formula was built. The three elements *didakton*, *askēton* and *physis* were already present, with *mathēton* as an obvious synonym for the first of these.

Greater systematisation is apparent when we turn to Aristotle, who usually avoided the awkward juxtaposition of nouns and adjectives which we saw in the *Meno*. It also seems that Aristotle was more conscious of the advantages of a particular order in the triad. Thus we find the following combinations:

physei, ethei, didachei	(*Ethica Nic.* 1179 b 20)
physis, ethos, logos	(*Politica* 1332 a 40)
physei, ethei, mathēsei	*Metaphysica* 1047 b 33)

An odd one out is the combination *ethesi, philosophiāi, nomois* (*Politica* 1263 b 40) though this too fits the general pattern. This was contained not in the actual words used, but in the significance attached to their position within the triad. First place was given to the constitutive principle, second to the corroborating testimony, third to the means of application. Stated in this form, the pedagogical triad soon became a commonplace of ancient philosophical thought. Direct evidence of Aristotelian influence is provided by Cicero, who wrote: *Ab Aristotele mores instituta disciplinas ... cognovimus* (*De fin.* 5.11). The passage is intriguing because in the literal sense, there is no corresponding phrase actually used by Aristotle. Even allowing for the uncertainties of translation, it seems hardly likely that Cicero would ever have put *mores* as the equivalent of *physis*. *Mores* is clearly *ethē*, but then what is *instituta*? This could be *nomoi* but that would leave us with the combination *ethē, nomoi, mathēseis* which is not attested in Aristotle. The 'translation' is explicable, however, if we assume that Cicero was referring primarily to a triadic scheme whose elements were all present in Aristotle, and not to a particular verbal formula. This is borne out by another passage, in which *mos* and *disciplina*, now in the singular, appear with *religio* as the second element (*De div.* 2.70).

By Cicero's time the idea of using triads had caught on in almost any context, and his writings are a rich source of supply. His rhetorical expertise occasionally produced inversions (or partial inversions) to vary the effect, but when this is taken into account, we are left with the following:

ingenio, usu, doctrina	(*De oratore* ii.39.162)
ingenio, doctrina, usu	(ibid., iii.20.77)
studio, ingenio, doctrina	(ibid., iii.4.16)
artis, studii, natura	(*De invent.* i.2)
ingenium, artem, usus	(*Pro Balbo* 20.45)
natura, usu, doctrina	(*Pro Scauro* 24)

From this it will be apparent that Cicero's writings show a high degree of verbal consistency, although even after due allowance has been made for the influence of rhetoric, a logical order in the elements is more difficult to discern. It is likely that he was not particularly bothered about this, since he was mostly speaking in practical terms about human qualities, although he had a certain tendency to put *ingenium* (which is to be identified with *natura*, cf. *De orat.* i.25.113) first and then *doctrina* and *usus*, either in that or in reverse order. The inversion of the second and third words is not as significant as it might appear, since the main emphasis fell on the first element of the triad, and other writers like Plutarch did the same (*De lib. educ.* 2a).

The hypothesis that *ingenium – natura – physis* was the con-

stitutive principle of this particular triad is confirmed by the
evidence of later writers. Taking them in turn we find the
following:

Plutarch:	*physis, logos, ethos*	(*De lib. educ.* 2a)
	physis, mathēsis, askēsis	(ibid., 3b)
Quintilian:	*natura, arte, exercitatione*	(iii.5.1)
	ingenii, doctrina, usu	(vi.2.3)
	natura, doctrina, studium	(vii.10.14)
	ingenii, studii, doctrinae	(xii.1.9)
Apuleius:	*ingenium, usus, disciplina*	(*De Platone* 228)
Marius Victorinus:	*natura, studio, disciplina*	(*Explan. in Cic. Rhet.*, Teubner, p. 156, 1)
Augustine:	*natura, disciplina, usus*	(*De div. quaest.* 83.q.38)
	natura, doctrina, usu	(*De civ. Dei* ii.25.5.22)
	physica, logica, ethica	(ibid.)

These examples, which range in date over four centuries, are
sufficiently uniform for us to be able to state with confidence
that a definite formula existed, based on the fundamentally
Platonic idea of nature.[26]

At the same time, however, there was another version of the
triad, which apparently owed more to Stoic influence than to
Plato. This variation on the common theme is also found in
Cicero, though probably it originated with Posidonius or with
another philosopher whom Posidonius copied. As the phrase
stands in the *De officiis* (1.156) it reads: *leges, mores, disciplinam.*
It appears again in reverse order in the *De re publica* (1.2) as
disciplinis, moribus, legibus. Plutarch claimed that all things could
be attributed to three causes, *nomos, ananke* and *ethos*[27] and there
is evidence, as in the examples quoted above, that he regarded
ethos and *askēsis* as interchangeable, at least in certain contexts.
The characteristic features of the 'Stoic' triad are that it re-
places nature with law as the first element, and shows a
preference for *disciplina* over *doctrina* or any of its synonyms.
Thus it is probable that the Ciceronian *mos, religio, disciplina* is

to be attached to the 'Stoic' branch of the triad although there are other instances, e.g. *voluntate, studio, disciplina* (*Flacc.* 53) where Platonic elements are stronger. The use of *disciplina*, therefore, is not a guarantee of Stoicism although it was characteristic of that school.

Of all the various forms of the triad which we have looked at so far, there is no doubt that the Ciceronian *leges, mores, disciplina* comes closest to the *Scriptura, natura, disciplina* which we find in Tertullian. The similarity is all the greater when we remember that for Tertullian Scripture was the *lex Dei* and as such was given pride of place. It also ties in well with what we know about Tertullian's sympathies with Stoicism. But do these resemblances, striking though they are, amount to proof that Tertullian borrowed his language from Cicero? Probably not. Cicero almost always preferred plural to singular nouns in his triads, and although it is not difficult to see why *Scriptura* should have replaced *leges*, *natura* is a much less likely equivalent for *mores*. More significantly, the pattern is wrong. *Natura* in Cicero usually came first in a triad, and never occurred with *leges*. Given the equation of *natura* with *ingenium*, it is extremely unlikely that Cicero, or the Stoics generally, would have regarded an irrational element as dependent on a well-ordered *nomos*. *Lex* could replace *ingenium*, conceivably even follow it (as an element of *ars* or *disciplina*), but it could not precede it. Tertullian may well have got some of his vocabulary from Cicero – given the history of Latin technical terms, this would have been difficult to avoid – but at a deeper level their thoughts ran in rather different channels.

Somewhat surprisingly, a closer parallel than anything Cicero offers can be found in Philo of Alexandria. To some extent Tertullian moved in a spiritual milieu not dissimilar to Philo's but it must remain doubtful whether he was acquainted with his works at first hand. He never mentioned Philo by name although that does not necessarily mean much. Hellenised Jewish converts to Christianity may have helped diffuse Philonic concepts to most parts of the Early Church, which may account for the wide spread of allegorising tendencies which Tertullian condemned so strongly. (On the other hand, he did recognise the need for allegorical interpretation in certain parts of the Old Testament, and this may have drawn him closer to Philo, whose exegetical methods were beginning to have a great influence on Clement of Alexandria and Origen.) But whatever the case may be, it is worth noting that Philo's triadic formula is both more stable in form than any of the philosophers', and closer to Tertullian's own. Philo uses the combination *mathēsis* (or, with approximately equal frequency, *didaskalia*), *physis*, *askēsis*. Variations of this pattern occur, but they are rare and insignificant.[28] It is hardly necessary to remind ourselves that for Philo, both *mathēsis* and *didaskalia* refer primarily to Scripture, the divine *mathēsis*, and *physis* is certainly closer to *natura* than either of these is to *mos*. Particularly important is the way in which Philo habitually put *mathēsis/didaskalia* before *physis*, a trait which marks him off as unique in the Greek-speaking world.[29] Nor is this a matter of indifference. Being a devout Jew, Philo could hardly admit that the instruction specifically given by God was in any way inferior to, or dependent upon, mere nature, which anybody could examine whether he had been enlightened by the Law or not. The subordination of nature to Scripture was a characteristically Judaeo-Christian phenomenon which stands out as such even when tinged, as in Tertullian's case, with elements derived from Stoicism.

The only major difficulty arises when we consider *disciplina* as a translation of *askēsis*. Cicero had of course used *disciplina* in his triads, but he explicitly claimed to have got his usage from Aristotle, and Aristotle avoided the word *askēsis* in favour of *didachē* or *mathēsis*. Philo, on the other hand, never used *didachē* in a triad, although *mathēsis* and *didaskalia* appear as synonyms. Quite why Philo used *askēsis* at all is hard to say. Protagoras and Plato had both used it, of course, but that was before triadic formulae had really been developed. Probably it is the simplest answer which is the most likely. Philo could not use *didachē* because it was synonymous with *mathēsis* and too similar in form to *didaskalia*, and so chose *askēsis* as the most suitable alternative. Stoic influence may also have played a role in this.

More to the point, it seems quite possible that Tertullian was thinking primarily of *askēsis* when using the word *disciplina*. The Latin term can be used to translate three different words in Greek, *didachē*, *paideia* and *askēsis*. The first of

these occurs in Cicero and the second in the Latin New Testament, but neither quite fits Tertullian's usage. New Testament
occurrences of *didachē* he translated not by *disciplina* but by
doctrina,[30] though Morel has argued that Tertullian often used
doctrina and *disciplina* synonymously, basing his case on the
frequency with which the two words occur in tandem.[31] But
it must be remembered that even this is no guarantee that the
two words are identical; *disciplina* was often used in contexts
where *doctrina* would clearly have been inappropriate, including the passage we are at present discussing. Tertullian did
use *disciplina*, on the other hand, to translate the New Testament *paideia*, which in turn is a translation of the Hebrew
mûsār.[32] Doubtless, *disciplina*, with its emphasis on learning the
hard way, was the best word to convey this idea in Latin, but
Tertullian used the term in ways which can scarcely be said to
correspond to *paideia* in the New Testament sense.[33]

A comparison of the two words shows that *disciplina* was much
too formalised a concept to accord well with *paideia*, which
strikes us as meaning rather a regrettable necessity in exceptional
circumstances. *Paideia* corresponds more closely to Tertullian's
correctio than to *disciplina* which with its complicated system of
regulated behaviour can only be described as a primitive form
of asceticism,[34] which of course makes a derivation from *askēsis*
all the more likely. The fact that *disciplina* stands for *paideia* in
Tertullian's New Testament quotations need not matter
unduly; it may well have been a traditional translation which
Tertullian was content to retain and subordinate to his own
somewhat different ideas.[35] On the whole, therefore, it seems
most consonant with the general tenor of his works to say that
mentally Tertullian was more akin to Philo than to Cicero or
Aristotle.

Thus we see how the triad of *Scriptura*, *natura* and *disciplina*
assumed its shape and substance. As in all such formulae, the
order in which the terms occurred had its own importance.
Scripture was the constitutive principle, the *point de départ*,
nature the corroborating witness, and discipline the practical
application. In the looser structure of the philosophers it was
usually possible for the second and third of these elements to
change places; as in a bar of music, the ictus fell at the beginning, and there was little concern to establish the precise value

of the rest. But for Tertullian such laxity was scarcely possible. Tied in with his triad was a complete theology. It was not chance or convenience which had established this system, but the Spirit of revelation himself. As we hinted earlier, it was the Father who gave the Law, the Son who confirmed it by taking on human nature, and the Spirit who applied it by discipline. Such a scheme of divine activity inevitably placed the last of the three at the very centre of the Church's concern. In the Pentecostal reign it was sanctification which the redeemed must pursue, and discipline, so the Holy Spirit had revealed, was the chosen means by which the Will of God would be accomplished.

CHAPTER FIVE

THE HOLY LIFE

We have seen how Tertullian constructed a theological system coloured by a latent ascetic bias, which enabled him to advocate a pattern of rigorous spiritual discipline in the Church. It is important to realise, however, that although Tertullian was undoubtedly a powerful and original thinker, many of the developments which he sought to encourage were not unknown elsewhere in the Oecumene. Recent investigation has made it clear that the late second century was a time of deepening spiritual ferment throughout the Roman world, a time moreover when Christianity first began to make itself felt as a serious rival to the pagan cults. As the new faith spread, it developed a fuller expression of tendencies latent in its own nature. In particular there was an increasing awareness among Christians of the element of voluntary renunciation connected with the perfect life of the resurrection.

In the New Testament there is a great deal of teaching about the second coming of Christ and the life of heaven, but in the canonical Scriptures these things are always balanced by careful reminders that the *parousia* has not yet come, and that for the time being Christians must be content to live in the tension of a revelation whose final goal has not yet been consummated. But as the Apostolic Age receded into history, this equilibrium was gradually lost by large sections of the Church. Most New Testament scholars believe that the *parousia* hope began to fade after the fall of Jerusalem in AD 70, but although there might be some truth in this view, there is much to suggest that in fact a very different development took place. All the evidence indicates that instead of abandoning the expectation of a new age, the second-century Church actually intensified this great hope. This showed itself in the tendency, well documented in the writers of this period, to apply biblical teaching about the resurrection life to present experience, in expectation of the imminence of the final consummation of all things.

It is quite possible that many subsidiary factors like Hellenistic dualism or a revulsion against the gross sexual immorality of some pagan cults contributed to the spread of Christian asceticism, but the main impulse and the staying power behind it could only have come from within Christianity. Thus the New Testament passages which stressed the Christian's rightful participation in the sinful temporal world were played down, and the demands of the end-time given new emphasis. At the practical level, this tendency was particularly evident in matters relating to matrimony. St Luke (20.35–6) records that Jesus said that 'those who are deemed worthy to take part in ... the resurrection of the dead neither marry nor are given in marriage ...', a remark which in the context could apply only to those whose mortal life had ceased, but which was extended by the early Christians to cover the living as well. In addition, St Paul's preference for celibacy (cf. 1 Cor. 7, etc.) was widely held to be an encouragement to the Church to move in the same direction.

Apocryphal writings of the second century abound in allusions to the superiority of the unmarried state, and there are occasional references to Adam's fall as the beginning of sexuality.[1] The great unsolved mystery in the origins of Christian asceticism is the extent to which similar practices in non-Christian religions and sects influenced its development. Philo has left us extended accounts of the Essenes of Judaea and the Therapeutae of Egypt, both of whom prefigure the monasticism of the Desert Fathers,[2] but whether or not either of these groups came into contact with Christians is unknown. It may be, as some have suggested, that the dominant strand in the primitive Syrian Church was a kind of Jewish Christianity influenced by the Qumran community, but great caution is required here. We must bear in mind that there were many variations within the ascetic movement, that encratism was often condemned in the earliest period, and that some of the most important figures like Bardaisan (Bardesanes) were apparently unaffected by the phenomenon.[3]

We have mentioned the Syrian Church specifically, because it provides us with the most detailed information about primitive asceticism and because the history of its origins has offered the most fruitful field for scholarly speculation. In particular, it is impossible to ignore the massive work of the Estonian scholar Arthur Vööbus, who has catalogued the rise of Syrian asceticism in great detail. Like Bauer before him, Vööbus was forced to deduce where he could not prove, with results which are sometimes unfortunate. For example, his study examines at some length the teachings of Marcion and Valentinus (both of whom were censured by Tertullian), and concludes that they exercised a powerful influence in Syria.[4] Against this possibility, however, must be weighed the fact that both men were expelled from the Church at an early date, and their condemnation was evidently accepted in Syria with as much conviction as elsewhere.[5] There is also little indication that Syrian asceticism followed Marcion in repudiating the Old Testament or that it indulged in the philosophical fantasies of the Valentinians.

Vööbus also gives great weight to the influence of Tatian, and here he may be on firmer ground. Converted about the middle of the second century and devoted to Justian Martyr, Tatian spent the early years of his Christian life at Rome, where many Syrians had established themselves.[6] Eventually, however, he grew dissatisfied with the Church there, which seemed to lack the rigour and sense of mission which had characterised the first preachers and martyrs. In AD 172 he broke with it and returned to Syria.[7] The West condemned him as a heretic, but in Syria his name is still revered as that of a great scholar and disciple of Justin.

According to Vööbus, Tatian encouraged a form of asceticism derived from the Gospels. His first demand was that men should renounce earthly honours and possessions (Tatian Oratio, ch. 11). Then came the restraints which must be put on bodily desires. Fasting and continence were obligatory, of course, and it seems that wine also was prohibited (cf. Jerome Comm, in Amos 2.12). It may be difficult to see how Tatian could have got all this from the Gospels, but we must remember that for him the main goal of the ascetic was to imitate the life of Christ even to the smallest details. It is interesting to note that he was prepared to tamper with the Sacred Text when he thought the original departed from the strictness of the ascetic ideal. Thus in St John 15.1 he altered Jesus' saying 'I am the vine' to 'I am the tree of the fruit of the earth', and similar adjustments can be found to his teaching on marriage as well.

Why did Tatian feel it was necessary to make these changes? Vööbus supposes that the main reason was that he was deeply impressed by the suffering of Jesus, and particularly by the warnings that his disciples, if they were to be true to his teaching, would have to carry their cross as well. Since the early life of Jesus was but the prelude to his death, everything told of it ought to be seen in this life. Passages which portrayed or hinted at an easy life detracted from the central message, and in Tatian's view were not part of Jesus' authentic teaching. It was in order to recover this that Tatian composed his Diatessaron, or harmony of the four Gospels, the first major attempt at a critical evaluation of the earliest Christian records.

If the ascetic life can be summed up in a few words, it was a holy war against the principalities and powers which ruled the world. Demons were very real to the ascetics, and influenced their thinking at least as much as the prospect of martyrdom. Jesus had warned men that it was more important to be on guard against those who could harm the spirit than against those who could touch the body only, and the feeling that here was a form of self-denial higher even than the cross or the arena became a standard feature of later monastic spirituality. The *martyrium perpetuum* of asceticism called for powers of endurance which those who were slain more swiftly did not require.

Tatian, however, did not restrict his use of imagery to warfare. St Paul had also spoken of the Christian life as a race whose prize was an eternal crown of glory. The spiritual athlete, like the soldier, could not afford to slacken the rigours of his training, and this apparently became a major justification for asceticism.

Prominent among the disciplines which Tatian expected his followers to practise was total abstinence from sexual intercourse. Carnal intercourse, whether for procreation or pleasure, was fornication.[9] Virginity was the highest of virtues, but lest a man or woman feel excluded from the discipline of sanctification because of past sins, Tatian was quick to point out that virginity could be practised in two separate forms. A man or woman could be a natural virgin, in which case he or she bore the name *bethula* (fem. *bethulta*), which in Syriac meant a person who had never enjoyed sexual intercourse. It was also possible, however, for a married couple to live in continence after conversion, in which case they were dignified with the name of *qaddishin*, holy ones.

This use of *qaddishin* is intriguing, because there does not seem to be an exact parallel to it anywhere else. Why should married couples living together in continence be considered 'holy', when natural virgins were not? Perhaps the answer can be found by contrast with the pagan religions of the region. From time immemorial Syria had been the home of cruel and debauched fertility cults, whose rites included ritual intercourse with one of the god's prostitutes, who were also called *qaddishin*.[10] What better way to show how diametrically opposed to all this Christian teaching was than by applying the same word to those who practised chastity within marriage? This might also explain how asceticism penetrated the popular consciousness so effectively. To the ordinary Syrian, sexual intercourse was bound up with his cult. To abandon the latter in favour of Christianity would inevitably make the former suspect as well. As a light in the heathen darkness, the Christian idea of holiness was the exact opposite of the commonly received notion.

Syrian Christianity, it should be remembered, never went so far as to condemn marriage altogether, although no true Christian was expected to indulge himself in this way. The words of Jesus about leaving a wife for his sake, and St Paul's recommendation of celibacy were not lost on the Syrians. To this end they developed a complex and spurious doctrine of *ihidayuta*, which arose out of a confusion in Syriac between *ihidaya* = *monogenēs* (only-begotten) and *ihidaya* = *monachos* (solitary). Christ himself was the *Ihidaya* (only-begotten) and to become an *ihidaya* (now in its other sense) was the highest form of Christian service. The believer must leave his family and dedicate himself to Christian celibacy, he must be single-minded in his resolve, and he must strive to put on the mind of Christ himself. In this doctrine was found the supreme theological and practical expression of the Syrian Fathers' ascetic teaching.

TERTULLIAN'S ASCETICISM

When we compare the findings of Vööbus with what we know of Tertullian's disciplinary injunctions, we are struck by the number of remarkable similarities between them, though we must not forget that there were also important differences. In our present state of knowledge it is impossible to say whether or not Tertullian was in touch with developments in Syria, or even to what extent practices well documented there in the fourth century were known as early as the second. If Vööbus is right in assigning such an important role to Tatian, then it is surprising that although he was mentioned by Irenaeus (*Adv. haer.* i.28.1), his name does not appear in Tertullian's writings and there is no indication that his teaching – if indeed it was his teaching – was known at Carthage. The fact that Tertullian readily publicised his knowledge of Montanus, who was a good deal more obscure and disreputable, makes a deliberate silence with respect to Tatian highly unlikely, if he in fact made use of his teaching. We ought to conclude, therefore, that this was probably not the case.

A serious comparison of their respective views confirms this initial judgment. Tatian's theological outlook, at least as represented by Vööbus, was primarily christocentric. Tertullian would probably not have been unsympathetic to a call to follow the *Ihidaya* (though, of course, the semantic confusion underlying this doctrine did not exist in Latin), but his own outlook was primarily pheumatocentric, and linked to a profound concern with the problem of time, a notion scarcely discernible in Syria.

At a more superficial level, Tertullian's use of imagery was also more restricted to the concept of warfare than it apparently was in Syria. There is only one instance in which he used the parallel of the Christian athlete (*Ad mart.* 3.3–4) and there is little specifically ascetic teaching connected with it. The military imagery, however, was much more frequent. Of course, many extenuating factors may have helped to account for this, e.g. the Romans were not particularly fond of games, Tertullian's father may have been a soldier,[11] and so on. But these cannot have been decisive. The crucial difference between a soldier and an athlete was that the former was an agent of the state, which in Roman eyes made him a much more revolutionary figure than a Christian athlete could ever be.

Moreover, when the Syrians spoke of holy warfare, they had in mind a spiritual battle against the demons which assaulted the soul in its human body. Tertullian did not reject this picture, but demonic powers were much less prominent in his thinking. In his writings the language of suffering and the soul's imprisonment have a decidedly worldly ring. It is significant that although his confessions of faith and his eschatological hope focus strongly on the return of Christ, they say nothing at all about the consummation of mystical union with him. For Tertullian the renewed life in the Spirit, who was at work both in individuals and in the Church, was a much more attractive proposition. Against the uncertainties and injustices of Roman rule, he could set the perfect reign of the Paraclete; to the state which claimed to embrace every man in its Oecumene, he could answer with the Church, a secret society perhaps, but one which had penetrated every corner of the pagan Empire and which would soon be revealed as the true ruler of the world (*Apol.* 1.6, *et passim*).

As for particular details, where Tatian apparently forbade the consumption of meat and wine because they were evil *in themselves*, Tertullian took a rather different line. He recognised that meat and wine were widely shunned by ascetics, but was cautious in forbidding their use. As far as he was concerned, it was not the substances which were evil, but the desire for them, a corruption which as Jesus had said, came not from outside the man but from within him. Adam after all had fallen, not because the fruit he ate was bad, but because he had succumbed to carnal lusts (*De ieiun.* 3.2). The same was true of marriage. Unlike Tatian, Tertullian did not say that carnal union was fornication in and of itself.[12] It was the human desire motivating sexual intercourse which was wrong and which had to be suppressed.

The shift of emphasis from the act to the intention behind it was of the greatest significance. Tertullian was aware, as the Syrians possibly were not, that the cause of sin went deeper than any evil inherent in matter. This also explains why Tertullian emphasised the role of the Holy Spirit in preference to the imitation of Christ, since the latter would inevitably get bogged down in externals. For him asceticism was an internal affair, and proceeded from a mind transformed by the Spirit. Virtue was not a matter of fanatical rejection but of reasoned restraint, governed by a will fortified with the indwelling presence of the Paraclete. The imitation of Christ was not lost sight of, but it was firmly tied to an acceptance of the incarnation and a recognition that the flesh and all created things were good in the sight of God.

For all these reasons, therefore, it is easy to understand why the Holy Spirit cult of Montanus appealed to Tertullian more than the *ihidayuta* ideal of the Syrians could ever have done. But can Montanism explain his asceticism? True, they had renounced earthly possessions in the expectation that the New Jerusalem was about to descend, but this was not asceticism in the true sense. Tertullian's own warnings about the approaching end were not only more sophisticated than this, they were aimed more at self-control than at outright abandonment of the world. Undoubtedly, Tertullian was deeply impressed by the Montanist spirit of self-denial, and thought their practices should be mandatory in the Church. But what the Montanists had done in a spirit of ecstasy, with no clearly defined purpose, Tertullian put on a rational theological foundation. It was the progressive unfolding of the revelation in time, not a chance vision or prophecy, which served him as a base for constructing a reasoned apology for his asceticism.

There is little evidence to suggest that Syrian or Phrygian asceticism influenced Tertullian directly, but there is a third possibility, which is that a common source may lie behind them all.[13] This source has been labelled 'Jewish Christianity' and given the widest interpretation by the late Cardinal Daniélou.[14] Daniélou's thesis is that the earliest Christian communities were heavily influenced by converts from Judaism, both orthodox and heretical, who have left us a number of superficially Christianised documents which are only now beginning to receive the attention their importance deserves.

What is of special significance for us is that Daniélou claims not only that this Jewish Christianity was widely influential in Syria, a thesis which can be given a certain *a priori* plausibility from the historical, linguistic and geographical links between that country and Palestine, but also that it had a particular importance in the Latin-speaking world. Daniélou mentions a number of minor writings, of which 5 *Esdras* and the *Passio Perpetuae et Felicitatis* are the best known, and finds in them evidence of tendencies which reflect this supposed influence.[15]

Superficially, his examination of these writings is so thorough that it appears to be conclusive, with the result that we must admit the existence of an influential Latin-speaking Jewish-Christian community during the greater part of the second century – well before Tertullian.

On the other hand, Daniélou's theory is not without its difficulties, and taken together, these make his case much less convincing. First, there is his arbitrary grouping of a number of short and mutually unconnected works under a single heading, and his dating of these works to the second century. The *Passio Perpetuae*, however, can hardly be this early, since the martyrdoms which it celebrates occurred in AD 203, and Daniélou's statement that Tertullian's *Scorpiace* is dependent on the *Adversus Iudaeos* (thereby supposedly giving AD 212 as a *terminus ante quem* for the later document) has no evidence to support it.[16]

Second, there is his extremely wide definition of what constitutes Jewish Christianity, which at one point reaches out to engulf most if not all the phenomena usually classed under that equally elastic heading 'gnosticism'. The result is that even the most casual allusion to a Judaic or quasi-Judaic practice can be pressed into service in support of his argument, with little or no regard for the widespread cultural syncretism of the second century or the possibility of an independent development.

Third, there is Daniélou's portrayal of Tertullian as a fundamentally anti-Judaic writer. From beginning to end Tertullian's works are supposed to show a constant *prise de position* against Judaeo-Christianity, as Daniélou has conceived it. Whether or not this is true – and from the reception which Daniélou's hypothesis has received, it would appear that most scholars have found it greatly exaggerated, to say the least – it certainly puts a damper on any suggestion that Jewish Christianity may have influenced his asceticism. It is particularly noteworthy in this connection that Tertullian never exploited the close affinities which existed between the Jewish and Roman understandings of human origins, though he was certainly aware of them and they were to play a significant role in later Christian apologetic.[17] It is true that he may have been marginally influenced by tendencies to which he was fundamentally opposed, but the balance of probabilities suggests that we must look elsewhere for a satisfactory explanation of his ascetic leanings. We believe that the most likely source for these lies not in oriental excesses, but in his own reaction to his pagan Roman past. Tertullian is often portrayed as the man who radically rejected even the more admirable elements in classical culture and religion. Much has been made, for instance, of his remark *Quid ergo Athenis et Hierosolymis?* (*De praescr. haer.* 7.9) which is supposed to reflect his uncompromising extremism in such matters. There is an element of truth in this, of course, but great care is needed to ensure that statements of this kind are properly understood. It is noticeable, for instance, that in his attacks on paganism, the examples chosen for explicit denunciation are all *Greek* in origin. *Roman* pagans came off generally very much better, and Seneca nearly acquired the status of an 'anonymous Christian' (*De anima* 20.1). At other times he recommended the constancy of the old Roman heroes as a model for Christians to follow (*Ad mart.* 4.4–9; *De mono.* 17.2–4) and the Vestal Virgins were always able to offer a challenge to the piety of Christian women (*De exhort. cast.* 13.2–4).

In his attitude to Roman religion, Tertullian took a line which must be considered ambivalent. Polytheism and extravagance he naturally abhorred, but much of the developed cult was of foreign importation. Authentic Roman religion, with its roots in the agrarian cycle of seed-time and harvest, birth and death, had a nobility which he admired and wished to see Christians bring to perfection. The secularism of Roman paganism, with its Virgilian yearning for a return to the blissful age of Saturn is reflected by Tertullian, who regarded the Pentecostal Age as the restoration of the primitive bliss of Eden (*De mono.* 4–5). Other Christians had seen this possibility in the Pauline imagery of Christ as the Second Adam, but none had gone so far as to make it the foundation of a complete eschatological social order. Pagan Rome must indeed be overthrown, but in its place would arise a new empire of the Spirit, to bring to perfection the noble ideals of the eternal city and its genius.

HOLINESS AND CHASTITY

The essential Romanness of Tertullian's ideals and outlook stands out clearly in his teaching on sanctification, particularly in its moral aspect. This qualification is necessary, since he recognised that in the realm of the intellect, which he regarded as primary, paganism had nothing to offer the Christian. The Roman influence is more apparent at the level of actual practice. Even the orthodox believer was confronted with the power of lusts within, and the need to fortify the flesh against temptation was high on the agenda of every spiritually minded Christian.

Bodily lusts revealed themselves in two basic desires – eating and sexual pleasure. In theory both were equally reprehensible, and fasting had a place alongside continence in Tertullian's scheme of sanctification. But there is only one treatise (*De ieiunio*) devoted to fasting, and in practice it occupies a much less prominent place than continence does. This imbalance can hardly have been due to the particular vices of Roman society, since according to Juvenal the Romans were great gluttons as much or even more than they were great lovers. Furthermore, there is little about the *De ieiunio* to give it a specifically Roman flavour. Much of it is taken up with xerophagy (the eating of dry food), clearly a foreign import, and Tertullian nowhere appeals to the fasting of ancient Roman heroes the way he does to their chastity.

The lack of attention given to fasting may well have been due to the fact that, as a religious exercise, it had little meaning in the Roman world, and neither Tertullian nor his readers would have made much of it. It was also a discipline which could never be perfected, since food was necessary for life quite apart from the lusts of the appetite (cf. *De anima* 38.3).

Continence, however, was quite another matter, and here the demands of asceticism were powerfully reinforced by Roman tradition and prejudice. There was an ancient link between holiness and chastity which is fully reflected in Tertullian's writings, where the terms *castitas* and *sanctitas* are frequently coupled. Lest it be thought that this was a coincidence arising out of Tertullian's Christian beliefs, we may recall to mind something of the history of the classical tradition.

The earliest literary evidence we have that the Romans frequently used *sanctus* and *castus* in tandem comes from Cicero, although there is a passage in Livy which suggests that the link may go back several centuries further in oral tradition. In a reference to the *ara pudicitiae plebeiae* (x.23.8) Livy said that it was attended '... *sanctius et a castioribus* ...' which suggests that even at that early date the Romans believed that there was a natural link between modesty and religious observance. Cicero certainly saw nothing unusual in coupling the two terms, as witness *De nat. deor.* 2.71 : '*cultus* ... *deorum est optimus idemque castissimus atque sanctissimus plenissimusque pietatis*'; or again, *De invent. rhet.* 2.144: '*praemia virtutis et officii sancta et casta esse oportere*'. It is true, of course, that Circero was not primarily interested in the moral aspect of these terms; he was much more concerned with ritual purity and correctness. This is clear from the way in which he applied the words indifferently to things and to people, paying no attention to their moral state. For instance, he wrote, *Pro Rab.* 11 : '*qui castam contionem, sanctum campum* ... *defendo servari oportere*' and *Pro Balbo* 9: '*quem ultimae gentes castiorem, moderatiorem, sanctiorem* [sc. *quam Pompeium*] *cogitaverunt?*'. In both these passages the meaning must surely be construed in a cultic rather than in a strictly moral sense.

After Cicero's time the application of *castus* and *sanctus* to inanimate objects seems to have died out, and the terms were used mainly to describe human beings. Thus we read in Manilius: '*si quem sanctum velis castumque probumque*' (4.571) and in Curtius: '*caste sancteque habitam esse reginam*' (iv.10.33). Pliny the Younger described Trajan as '*castus et sanctus et dis simillimus princeps*' (*Paneg.* 1.3), an interesting passage because it suggests that a man with these qualities was more godlike. *Castus* was frequently used to described a participant in a religious exercise, and of priests in general. In this connection it was often associated with *pius* rather than *sanctus*, although examples of the latter combination may also be found, as in Vitruvius i.7.2: '*religiose caste sanctisque moribus is locus debeat tueri*'; or Columella xii.18.4: '*sacrificia* ... *quam sanctissime castissime facienda*'. Aulus Gellius even described a priest as: '... *castitate vitae sanctus*' (xv.18.2).

It may be objected that in none of these instances is there any clear indication that sexual abstinence was implicit in *castitas*, but this objection must give way before the clear testimony of the classical writers who used both words together in contexts where female chastity was certainly what was meant. Tibullus, for instance, pleaded with Delia:

> At tu casta, precor, maneas, sanctique pudoris
> adsideat custos sedula semper anus.   (i.3.83–4)

A century and a half later we find Pliny the Younger praising the old-fashioned virtue of Fannia, wife of Helvidius: '*Doleo eam feminam maximam eripi oculis civitatis, nescio an aliquid simile visuris. Quae castitas illi, quae sanctitas, quanta gravitas, quanta constantia.*' (vii.19.4).

Furthermore this ideal of female chastity was firmly enshrined in Roman religion, as we can see from the honour paid to the Vestal Virgins. In their cult the ritual cleansing of the body was unmistakably associated with perpetual virginity. Physical virginity had special importance because unlike other forms of ritual chastity, once it had been defiled it could not be restored. The holiness of a Vestal Virgin was evident not from the correct performance of cultic observances, but from the physical fact of her virginity. Pliny the Younger makes this abundantly clear when he says of a Vestal who had betrayed her trust: '*foedum ... contactum quasi plane a casto puroque corpore novissima sanctitate reiecit*' (iv.11.9). We know from *De exhortatione castitatis* 13 that Tertullian certainly had Vestal Virgins in mind in his exhortations to chastity, and in the light of this it is not surprising to find that he ascribed perfect holiness to virgins (*Ad uxor.* i.8.2) and advocated virginity as the highest, though not the only, form of sanctification open to the Christian (*De exhort. cast.* 1.3–5).

Tertullian was also well acquainted with the old Roman notion that chastity in the form of continence within marriage was a special duty incumbent on priests and religious officials. Indeed, he explained these strict marriage laws and the occasional celibacy found among the pagan priesthood as a counterfeit of the divine ordinance (*Ad uxor.* i.7.5). This divine ordinance supposedly formed part of the levitical laws governing the marriage of Jewish priests, although in fact no such injunction exists (*De exhort. cast.* 7.3). There can be little doubt that in his equation of holiness with chastity, Tertullian was following closely in the mainstream of Roman thought from earliest times. This is all the more striking in that there is no exact parallel to the Roman idea either in the Greek or in the Judaeo-Christian tradition, despite Tertullian's sometimes desperate attempts to support his case from Scripture.

Of all the many passages which he quoted in his defence, none is more pointed than 1 John 3.3, which appears in *De monogamia* 3.7 as follows: '*Et omnis . . . qui spem ipsam in illo habet, castificat se, sicut et ipse castus est.*' The Greek original of this verse reads: *kai pas ho echōn tēn elpida tautēn – hautōi hagnizei heauton kathōs ekeinos hagnos estin.* The rendering of *hagnos* as *castus*, as far as we can judge, was Tertullian's own. Unfortunately there is no parallel text of the Vetus Latina extant, and the Vulgate translates *hagnos* as *purus* in this passage, although Jerome did use *castam* as a translation of *hagnēn* in 2 Corinthians 11.2, where the Church is described as a pure virgin. Interestingly enough, when Tertullian alluded to this passage he translated *hagnēn* as *sanctam* (*Adv. Marc.* v.12.6), which underlines our contention that the two words were virtually interchangeable. Tertullian's alternation between them as translations for the New Testament *hagnos* is not in itself surprising, as we shall see. What is more than questionable, however, is whether there was any genuine precedent for interpreting the meaning of *hagnos* in the restricted sense of 'chaste' which Tertullian evidently ascribed to *castus* and therefore, by virtue of association, to *sanctus* as well.

The word *hagnos* can be found in the earliest Greek literature and seems originally to have meant 'provoking a religious awe'. There is some doubt as to the exact meaning of the word in Homer, but there is at least one instance (*Od.* xi.386) where *hagnos* was applied to Persephone and cannot have had the meaning 'chaste'. Eduard Williger[18] has demonstrated that in pre-classical times *hagnos* was constantly used in the sense of 'taboo' though before long this was weakened to something corresponding to our word 'holy', especially as applied to things. Later, in Attic tragedy, we see the development of a secondary sense, 'ritually clean, pure'. It came to be virtually synonymous with *katharos*, and was frequently coupled with it in later Greek literature. It was especially frequent in the tragedians in the sense of 'free of blood-guilt'. Gradually the primitive meaning was lost sight of and *hagnos* came to mean simply 'clean' without any religious overtones. If it differed at all from *katharos* it is that it was used of cleansing by *water* whereas *katharos* was cleansing by *fire*. As for the meaning 'chaste', this is attested only rarely. Aristotle (*An. hist.* i.488 b 5) divided the animals into two categories, *aphrodisiastika* and *hagneutika*, and Williger claims that there was a popular custom of giving prostitutes the ironical name *Hagnē* (ibid., p. 72).

Hagnos did not appear again in a strictly religious context until the Septuagint, where it was used to mean 'ritually clean'. In particular the verbal form *hagnizein* was used to translate the Hebrew root *qdš* in the *Pi'el*, *Hiph'il* and *Hithpa'el*, when the meaning was 'to consecrate by purification'. The Hebrew word is infrequent, occurring only nineteen times, of which twelve are in 2 Chronicles 29–31. The Greek translators, however, were consistent in rendering it as *hagnizein*, which strongly suggests that the word was meant to convey the idea of sanctification by ritual cleansing. In the New Testament this idea is applied to the soul, as in 1 Peter 1.22: *tas psychas hymōn hēgnikotes en tēi hypakoēi tēs alētheias*. Similar ideas may be found in post-biblical Christian literature of the first and second centuries, where *hagnos* is used without any reference to chastity. As examples we may cite 1 Clement 1.3 which says: *en amōmō kai semnēi kai hagnēi syneidēsei* or again, the Epistle of Barnabas 8.3 which reads: *tēn aphesin tōn hamartiōn kai ton hagnismon tēs kardias*. This is likewise the meaning in 1 John 3.3 which Tertullian quoted, giving *hagnos* as *castus*. However, even in the few passages where *hagnos* undoubtedly did mean 'chaste', there is every reason to suppose that the word denoted a purity which was primarily spiritual rather than physical. As evidence of this we may cite Polycarp, who says (*Ep.* 5.3): *tas parthenous en ... hagnēi syneidēsei peripatein*. When physical chastity was meant it was spelled out in terms so obvious that it is difficult to believe that *hagnos* alone would ever have had the peculiar force of 'chaste'. A good example is 1 Clement 38.2 which reads: *ho hagnos en tēi sarki ... mē alazoneuesthō ginōskōn hoti heteros estin ho epichorēgōn autōi tēn enkrateian*. Clement seems to have felt it necessary to stress *en tēi sarki*. Furthermore there is no evidence that the Greeks ever linked *hagnos* with *hagios*, despite their ancient etymological connection. *Hagnos* was frequently coupled, not with *hagios* but with *katharos*, a fact which was doubtless reflected in the Vulgate's preference for *purus* in 1 John 3.3. Whilst it is possible to find Greek precedents for the use of *hagnos* to mean both 'chaste' and 'holy', it cannot be claimed that these were the standard meanings of the word. We may confidently assert, therefore, that Tertullian's coupling of *castus* meaning 'chaste' and *sanctus* had no ready equivalent in Greek.

For the record we may add that what was true of Greek in this respect was even more true of Hebrew. Not once in the Old Testament do we find *qdš* being used in connection with chastity or sexual continence within marriage. On the contrary, we find the word *q^{e}dēšâh* used to denote a temple prostitute (Gen. 38.21–2; Deut. 23.17; Hos. 4.14). Sexual abstinence for a time was the rule during special periods of fasting and prayer, but even in the New Testament this was regarded as purely temporary, and there was no special virtue attached to it outside the context of a particular observance. Tertullian certainly made use of Jewish precedent to support his case, but it is clear that however much he may have insisted that chastity was merely an aid to the worship of God, he esteemed it for its own sake as well, a fact which is sufficient to set him apart from writers in the Jewish tradition. In later Judaism there were men like Aristeas (cf. *Ep.* 139) who spoke of being *hagnoi … kata sōma*, but this was a ritual concept which did not necessarily imply chastity. Likewise the *Mishnah*, despite its preoccupation with ritual cleanliness, did not include virginity in this (cf. iii. *Yeb.* 6.6).

It would seem to be clear from this, therefore, that the close relationship between holiness and chastity which we find in Tertullian's writings bears the stamp of a Latin, rather than a Greek or Hebrew origin. If this suggestion is correct, then it is clear that Tertullian regarded Christian moral teaching as the natural fulfilment of pagan Roman beliefs, as well as of the Old Testament law. Their gods may have been false, and their theological understanding seriously distorted, but in the matter of morals at least, the precepts of the ancient Romans were worthy of emulation by Christians (*De exhort. cast.* 1.4).

Of course it should be emphasised that the approval given to pagan customs was conditional on their conformability to fundamental Christian precepts, and was not merely the baptising of a heathen religion. When pagan habits conflicted with Christian teaching it was the former, not the latter, which gave way. Thus, for example, the Roman ideal of chastity was closely linked to the cult of the family, which lay at the heart of the traditional religion. Even the state was conceived in terms of an extended family, as witness the title *pater patriae* which was borne by Augustus and his successors. Devotion to the family, however, meant that great importance was attached to procreation as the means by which the line might be perpetuated and the worship of the hearth gods carried on. To the Roman mind immortality was understood in terms not dissimilar to what we would call ancestor worship, and the aim of the Roman was to have as many descendants as possible to perpetuate his memory.

Such a religion, however, could hardly be tolerated by Tertullian, since it obviously interfered with Christian ideas of virginity and life-long continence. It betrayed a lack of faith in the imminence of the *parousia* when time would be gathered up and brought to an end. For this reason he denounced the procreation of children as inconsistent with true faith, and urged married couples to remain childless (ibid.). Christian chastity was not intended to preserve the honour of the family, but to glorify the Lord of heaven and earth.

THE SEVERAL STATES OF CONTINENCE

It was a matter of universal agreement among ancient ascetics that continence was an essential aspect, even perhaps the foundation, of the truly holy life. But the pressures of practical reality obliged even the most rigorous of them, at any rate in the earlier period, to recognise that there was more than one form which abstention from sexual intercourse could take. Both in Syria and in North Africa we can trace the development of a certain diversity in the practice of virginity from the very start. In Syria there were two forms of continence which were widely diffused in the Church. The first of these was *betuluta*, or virginity in the strict sense. Alongside this there was the practice of *qaddishuta*, which strictly speaking meant 'holiness' in Syriac, but which was used exclusively of married couples who had

taken the vow of continence. Vööbus' remarks on this subject
(op. cit., p. 72) are worth quoting:

> This word [*qaddishuta*] refers to sexual continence so that
> 'holy' is used as a synonym for chastity and purity. But it
> also must be observed that this term is distinctly separated
> from *betuluta*, virginity, which expression is reserved to those
> women and men who have kept their virginity and not
> married. The term 'holiness' then refers to married couples
> who have not preserved their virginity but practice con-
> tinence. This practice can be noted clearly in *De virginitate* as
> well as in other ancient documents.

When we turn from this to Tertullian's teaching, the first
thing which strikes us is the absence of the distinction between
virginitas and *sanctitas* which apparently existed in Syria. Instead,
Tertullian distinguished three grades of abstinence, all of which
he designated as holy and two of which (at least) constituted
virginity as well (*De exhort. cast.* 1.4). In his teaching the three
forms of continence were distinguished. First, there was natural
virginity, similar to the Syriac *betuluta*. This was the state of
blessed innocence, a happy condition to be in, but not especially
meritorious from God's point of view. Tertullian considered it
to be the easiest option to endure, since there was no real hard-
ship in forgoing what one had never known (ibid., 1.5). Natural
virginity might even be dangerous since if it were pressed to its
logical conclusion it might lead to the downgrading of the
institution of marriage, an eventuality which Tertullian regarded as heresy (*De mono.* 1.1). On the other hand, however,
he praised virginity in fulsome terms and stated that virgins,
thanks to their total commitment to chastity, enjoyed complete
fulfilled holiness (*De vir. vel.* 2.1; *Ad uxor.* i.8.2; *De exhort. cast.*
9.4).

On the surface these statements appear to contradict one
another, but each must be understood in its context. The holiness of innocence was indeed a wonderful thing, but as it was
a natural gift to all men at birth, no one had the right to claim
any merit for it. Since its virtue rested on ignorance, it could
not be applauded without a certain reserve. It must also have
been a rare phenomenon. Most of the people to whom Tertullian addressed himself, and indeed he himself, could not

claim this absolute virginity. But were they then to be excluded from the grace of sanctification? Certainly not! If only the innocent could know true holiness, then only Adam before the fall had any hope of salvation. Ignorance may have been a blessed state, but no Christian could suppose that it was superior to the life of those who had been redeemed and restored in Christ.

The second form of continence was more complex. This Tertullian described as virginity from the second birth (i.e. baptism' either by contract (in the case of married couples or by choice (in the case of the widowed). The logic of this was that when a man was baptised his previous life was wiped out and he could begin again from scratch. The waters of baptism restored the virginity which his pre-Christian sinfulness had lost. It is not clear whether this form of continence had an exact parallel in Syria or not. Probably candidates for baptism received instruction in the demands of the ascetic life, but we do not know to what extent this was integrated into a comprehensive theology of baptism and post-baptismal sin. Given the mystical leanings of the Syriac fathers and their distaste for precision in such matters, we shall probably never be able to answer the question with any degree of assurance.[19] It seems likely, however, that *qaddishuta* was advocated for married couples without particular reference to baptism, and is therefore not directly analogous to the practice Tertullian favoured.

The third form of continence which Tertullian advocated was the voluntary renunciation of sexual intercourse by married couples some time after baptism. The lapse of time between baptism and renunciation was not specified, but it is difficult to see how the third form of continence would have differed from the second if there were not some such interval. This conversion of carnal marriage into spiritual union more nearly parallels the Syriac *qaddishuta*, where the use of the word 'holy' served to emphasise the act of consecration rather than the state of continence itself. It differed from the Syrian convention, however, in the importance which Tertullian accorded it within his threefold scheme. In Syria the latent notion of abandonment which ran through all ascetic discipline meant that the *qaddishin* soon came under suspicion, since cohabitation was held to be inconsistent with the solitary life of the *ihidaya*.[20] In Tertullian's thinking, however, monogamous continence was the most important, if not actually the highest form of continence. As far as he was concerned, the greater the temptation, the nobler the virtue that resisted it (*De ieiun.* 4.4). He expressly forbade married couples to divorce, but urged them to live together in continence, praising God and helping each other to grow in the faith (*Ad uxor.* ii.1). Such a marriage, consecrated *spiritaliter in Christo*, to use Tertullian's phrase, would survive even death.

The doctrine of eternal marriage marked a new departure in Tertullian's thought, and one which landed him in considerable exegetical difficulty. Yet it is not hard to see the logic of his case. For if Christ had come to restore all things to the beginning and Adam had been married before the fall, how could it be admitted that marriage would cease to exist in the new creation (*Ad uxor.* i.3.2; *De exhort. cast.* 5.2; *De mono.* 4.2)? That Tertullian would push his doctrine of the essential goodness of matrimony to such an extreme is clear evidence, if any more were needed, of just how far he differed from Tatian, to whom any form of marriage was undesirable. Nevertheless, it must be admitted that Tertullian's teaching on eternal matrimony was developed primarily in order to combat the tendency of widows to look for another husband instead of giving themselves over to God completely.

How widespread this problem was is impossible to say, but there must have been many in the Church who had lost a partner in relatively early age. Tertullian himself may well have been one of them, although we cannot be sure about this.[21] In any case there can be no doubt that in rejecting the possibility of remarriage after the death of a spouse, he was led by progressive stages to develop a theory of the divine significance of the initial marriage vow. In *Ad uxorem*, for instance, he adopted a negative attitude to the whole idea of matrimony and declared flatly that there would be no marriage in heaven (*Ad uxor.* i.1.5). Later on, however, his tone changed considerably. Gone was the confident assertion that the woman with seven husbands would have no spouse waiting for her at the resurrection (*De mono.* 9.1). A Christian must understand that the *indulgentia* by which multiple marriage had existed prior to the sending of the Spirit had been withdrawn at Pentecost, and a better system installed in its place (ibid., 11.7).

A widower could thus take comfort in that his wife was separated from him in body but not in spirit (*De exhort. cast.* 11.1). The separation of death was only temporary; both partners would be reunited in heaven, in fulfilment of God's promise not to separate those whom he had joined together (*De mono.* 10.6). Furthermore, since Tertullian firmly believed in the resurrection of the body, it was a corporeal reunion which he envisaged (cf., ibid., 10.5). Purified of lust, the reunited couple would enjoy the same bliss as Adam and Eve had known in Eden.[22]

Having said all this, however, it remains true that Tertullian's attitude to marriage was never one of wholehearted approval. At bottom he believed that although God had undoubtedly created the institution, he had done so as a sop to the infirmity of the flesh (*Ad uxor.* ii.8.6–9; *De exhort. cast.* 12.2). This did not make it wrong in itself, especially as long as no higher form of life was recommended, but it did mean that matrimony was originally designed as an attempt to ward off worse evils rather than as a positive good. Thus St Paul was right when he said that it was better to marry than to burn, but that it was still better not to marry at all (*Ad uxor.* i.3.3; *De exhort. cast.* 3.9–10; *De mono.* 3.5). The fact that marriage was lawful did not matter; it was not expedient (*De exhort. cast.* 8.1). The demands of the Kingdom were too pressing to allow any time to be spent in such wasteful frivolities as marriage (ibid., 8.12). It is true that much of his argument was directed against the practice of remarriage, or digamy, but its force was felt by single Christians as well. Like the widowed, they were best advised to remain in the state in which they had been called (*Ad uxor.* i.4.3–5; ii.2.3; *De vir. vel.* 3).

HERETICS AND PSYCHICI

The attack on Tertullian's carefully constructed scheme came from two diametrically opposed directions. On the 'left' were the heretics who rejected marriage altogether; on the 'right' the *psychici* who regarded it as a purely temporal ordinance and permitted remarriage after a partner's death (*De mono.* 1.1). Unfortunately neither category is particularly well defined in his writings and we are obliged to reconstruct what we can from the evidence available to us. The heretics in particular are never clearly singled out, although it seems most likely that Tertullian had Marcion and his disciples in mind (cf. *Adv. Marc.* iv.11.6–9). On the other hand, he may have been thinking primarily of the dissidents whom St Paul had been obliged to reprimand (cf. 1 Cor. 7), in which case his introduction to the *De monogamia* must be construed as anachronistic. This, however, is unlikely. The third possibility is that he may have been motivated by a desire to refute charges of heresy laid against himself. This view is strengthened by the fact that he did not indulge in long tirades against the heretics, and his rejection of divorce, though it was somewhat lengthy, betrays a greater preoccupation with self-defence than with the need to refute unsound teaching on the part of others.[23] It is probable, therefore, that whoever these heretics may have been, and whatever Tertullian's motives were in denouncing them, they were not a large or influential body in the Church. Had things been otherwise we should expect to find a much more extensive refutation of their views.

In this respect the case of the *psychici* offers a remarkable contrast. Not only is far more space devoted to them, but we have a much better idea who they were – the main leaders of the Western Church, and in particular the Bishop of Rome.[24] A very large part of Tertullian's treatises on marriage is in fact taken up with a detailed examination of Scripture passages which the *psychici* used to defend their position. In his rebuttal Tertullian stretched all his considerable resources of argument and exegesis, although in the end he was unable to make a convincing case and fell back on secondary arguments which only highlighted the intrinsic weakness of his position.

The argument between Tertullian and the *psychici* seems to have been conducted along fairly straightforward lines, with each side producing proof-texts from Scripture which would then be refuted by the other side and counter-texts put forward. One obvious passage which supported the *psychici* was St Paul's advice that it was better to marry than to burn – *melius est nubere quam uri* (1 Cor. 7.9). As we have already mentioned, Tertullian countered this not so much by an appeal to other parts of Scripture as by an exercise in grammatical logic, from which he deduced that marriage, according to St Paul, was no more than the lesser of two evils. Elsewhere he was obliged to adopt more devious exegetical methods. He could not deny, for instance, that in the Genesis account of creation God had told man to be fruitful and multiply and replenish the earth, a passage which the *psychici* were evidently fond of using against him (*De exhort. cast.* 6.1–3; *De mono.* 7.3–4). Tertullian replied by appealing to his dispensational theories, according to which the original command had been fulfilled under the old law and no longer had any relevance (*De exhort. cast.* 6.3).

More significant than these, however, was the argument in favour of second marriages which the *psychici* based on 1 Corinthians 7.39, and which Tertullian never successfully refuted, despite many attempts to do so. The original Greek reads as follows:

gynē dedetai eph' hoson chronon zēi ho anēr autēs. ean de koimēthēi ho anēr eleuthera estin ho thelei gamēthēnai monon en Kyriōi.

This verse appears in three separate translations in Tertullian's works:

Ad uxorem ii.2.3–4:   *mulier defuncto viro libera est; cui vult nubat, tantum in Domino.*

De monogamia 11.3:   *mulier vincta est in quantum temporis vivit vir eius; si autem mortuus fuerit, libera est, cui vult nubat, tantum in Domino.*

De monogamia 11.10:   *mulier vincta est quamdiu vivit vit eius, si autem dormierit, libera est, cui volet nubat, tantum in Domino.*

In the first of these passages Tertullian was mainly concerned to demonstrate that Scripture forbade the marriage of a Christian with an unbeliever, and was therefore content to paraphrase the first half of the verse. He did add, however, that it was the will of the Holy Spirit that widows and the unmarried should remain as they were, although the more pressing question of mixed marriages rather pushed this advice into the background (*Ad uxor.* ii.2.4).

The full argument appeared only in the *De monogamia*. Tertullian had to grant the claim of the *psychici* that St Paul did in fact allow second marriages, but he insisted that this permis-

ion had been given in specific and unusual circumstances, and
that it had subsequently lapsed. To prove this, Tertullian
advanced a wide range of considerations. In the first place, he
claimed, the Corinthians whom St Paul had advised were new
Christians unable to endure the solid food of sound teaching
and still in need of a mother's milk (*De mono.* 11.6). For this
reason certain concessions had been granted to them along lines
already familiar to us, by the application of divine *indulgentia*
ibid., 11.7). Secondly, Tertullian maintained that St Paul was
speaking to Christians who had married before their conversion
and were now wondering whether to seek divorce. St Paul had
forbidden this, according to the law, but at the same time he
had laid down the principle that a man should not touch a
woman. Tertullian argued from this that the overriding
principle of 1 Corinthians 7 was that a man should remain in
the state in which he had been called. Permission to remarry
had been granted by the Apostle only to those who were widows
at the time of their conversion. They could take a 'second'
husband because becoming a Christian meant entering a
new life and the previous marriage did not count. In practice,
however, this permission was overruled by other considerations. The perils of the age and the imminence of the end
meant that it was more important to care for the things of
God than for the things of man, particularly the needs of a
husband.

Exegetically Tertullian's argument that only a converted
widow could remarry depended on the temporal force of the
Greek *ean de koimēthēi*. In classical Greek composition *ean* with
the subjunctive denoted either a present or a future condition,
and the aorist had no temporal significance. But Tertullian
apparently insisted that the subjunctive referred explicitly to
past time, and gave the translation 'if her husband be dead'
rather than 'if her husband should die'. What is the true meaning? In all probability both are possible, though Tertullian's
exclusion of the latter sense would be neither justified nor very
likely in Classical prose. This does not necessarily mean that his
knowledge of Greek was imperfect, however. It is quite possible
that he seriously believed that a future meaning was impossible,
not on the basis of Classical grammar, but according to contemporary demotic usage, where the earlier distinctions had

been erased and the subtleties of classical construction for
gotten. It is at least possible that we have here an indication
that Tertullian's use of Greek had not been influenced by the
neo-Atticism which was gaining ground in the Greek-speaking
world.[25] But however that may be, the argument was hardly a
good one, and it need not surprise us that it failed to convince
anybody.

Elsewhere, in the *De exhortatione castitatis*, Tertullian pu
forward an even more ingenious argument against second mar
riage by claiming that St Paul's advice on the subject was given
out of his own head, whereas his exhortations to chastity carried
divine authority. He claimed that the Apostle had advised
widows to be content with their lot, but if they remarried there
was nothing sinful in it (*De exhort. cast.* 4.1). St Paul had then
gone on to add that God had given him no direct command
in the matter, and that his advice was from one who was writing
out of faith and trust in the divine mercy (1 Cor. 7.25). But for
Tertullian, pressed as he was by the *psychici*, such an equivoca
tion was not good enough. There was all the difference in the
world between the commands of God and the precepts of men
Since there was no instance in Scripture where God himself
allowed a second marriage, and since what God did not allow
was automatically forbidden (a principle taken from Roman
law), remarriage was obviously not permitted. He then re
iterated his arguments from expediency, adding for good
measure that even first marriages were less than safe (*De exhort*
cast. 4.3). The argument was crowned with a quotation from
St Paul to the effect that a man would be happier if he
remained celibate like the Apostle. Tertullian then pointed ou
that this last remark was more than a mere opinion, since i
was followed by the Apostle's *puto autem, et ego Spiritum Dei habeo*
In direct contradiction to what we find in the *De pudicitia* he
did not apply this remark to the whole passage, which would
then have included the permission given to remarry, but re
stricted it to this one saying (ibid., 4.4–5).

The subtlety of these arguments and the shoddy exegesis
which accompanied them give a clear indication of just how
desperate Tertullian was in his attempts to override the obvious
statements of Scripture. There is at least one example, however,
where he went even further. This was in his argument drawn

from the nature of the priesthood. According to him, the levitical priests had been forbidden to remarry, in proof of which he quoted a non-existent passage from Leviticus.[26] Of course, Tertullian then hastened to point out that under the new dispensation all the faithful were priests, which meant that they were all subject to the spurious levitical discipline!

Apparently some churchmen were prepared to compromise with Tertullian on this issue. They would agree that eternal monogamy was binding on bishops, as St Paul had decreed (1 Tim. 3.2–7), but not on the laity. To this halfway measure Tertullian replied with a withering attack. According to him, such a compromise solution was nothing but the thin edge of the wedge (*subtilissima argumentatio*); it was the duty of the bishop to set an example for everyone else (*De mono.* 12.2). There could be no question of admitting digamy by the back door as it were, by allowing it to non-office holders.

A study of Tertullian's views on marriage inevitably raises difficult questions about the validity of his exegetical methods.[27] It is only too easy to assume that his interpretation of Scripture shows an authoritarian cast of mind which failed to appreciate the flexibility of St Paul's approach. But such a judgment would be far too severe. It is not true, for instance, that he ignored St Paul's broad tolerance of marriage and suppressed those parts of the Apostle's teaching which he did not like. On the subject of second marriages, for example, he was quite willing to admit that St Paul had allowed them, and insisted only that this concession be understood in its proper context. Permission to remarry had been granted, Tertullian argued, by divine *indulgentia*. During the time of waiting which preceded the final perfecting of the saints, a Christian might take a second partner if it were the only way to prevent worse evils, but this was not part of God's normative will. But now, Tertullian claimed, this time was rapidly coming to an end. The *parousia* was at hand, and this made the interim arrangements which the apostles had made largely obsolete (cf. *De exhort. cast.* 8.3, *et passim*).

Does this eschatological interpretation of marriage bear any relation to what St Paul actually taught? The problem is complicated today by the intense interest which his views on marriage, and on women in general, have aroused in the Church.

At the present time it is probably true to say that the teaching of 1 Corinthians 7 in particular is among the most unpopular and contested in the entire New Testament. Some have simply rejected it altogether, but this option is hardly possible for the committed Christian, for whom the Scriptures remain the final authority in matters of faith. As a result, there has been an increasing desire in recent years to interpret these passages as peculiarly relevant to their own age, but no longer applicable in quite the same way today. In support of this view it may be argued that St Paul was writing in the context of actual or impending persecution (cf. 1 Cor. 7.26) and that in other circumstances (such as our own?) he would have counselled a more positive approach to marriage.

This view is understandably attractive to those who cannot accept the permanent validity of the texts as they stand, but there can be no doubt that it involves a reinterpretation of St Paul far more drastic than anything Tertullian may have contemplated. The recent revival of interest in apocalyptic literature has shed new light on the implications of the word *ananke* ('distress', cf. ibid.) and confirmed the traditional eschatological interpretation of this text. St Paul clearly regarded marriage as a temporal institution, and therefore sought to put it in its context as a relative good, subordinate to spiritual things in the life of the Christian. In this respect Tertullian's mistake was not that he misunderstood St Paul, but that he tried to make the *eschaton* a present reality, in the belief that the end of time would then arrive.

Had Tertullian done no more than try to wind up history in the light of the apocalyptic events of his own time, it would be difficult to accuse him of a serious departure from Apostolic teaching, except in so far as the Apostles set no time-limit on their prophecies. More important were the consequences which flowed from Tertullian's presupposition. For the imminence of the *parousia* necessitated the Church's immediate and total sanctification *before* it arrived. It is here that major differences between Tertullian and St Paul begin to appear. The different conceptions of the 'flesh' and Tertullian's readiness to equate holiness with chastity need not have mattered very much if the final consummation of the Christian's vocation was relegated to eternity. It was the attempted secularisation of the *eschaton* which finally betrayed Tertullian's theology, and which allowed elements of pagan thinking to creep into his thought and ultimately vitiate it.

When we look at Tertullian's attitude from a distance of 1750 years and more it is easy enough to point to its inadequacies, its short-sightedness and its ultimate failure in the light of history. At the time, however, things must have seemed very different. Tertullian knew, if only subconsciously, that the Apostolic Age was gone beyond recall. The precise limits of the New Testament canon might still be disputed, but everyone agreed that new books would not be forthcoming. By his day, moreover, missionaries had made every nation conversant with the claims of Christ, so that pagan ignorance was no longer innocent as it had once been, but deliberate (*Apol.* 1.6–8). The Roman Empire had little to offer. Its bankrupt religions looked ridiculous beside Christianity, which suffered a totally unjustified persecution. The political settlement of Nerva's reign had been shattered in the civil strife of AD 193–7, and with it had gone the myth of an eternal *pax romana*. Can we wonder at the strength of Tertullian's eschatological vision?

Yet whatever excuses may be mustered in his defence, Tertullian was clearly wrong, and this was recognised by his contemporaries as much as it has been by subsequent generations. It is true that nobody wrote long treatises against him; his condemnation as a heretic was slow in coming and had little effect. But at the same time, no one very important rushed to his defence, although he seems to have had a considerable influence on the North African Church at the popular level.[28] Nor is this surprising. Much of what Tertullian had to say could be easily reduced to a few catch-phrases and widely disseminated to simple people uninterested in the subtleties of theological debate.[29] At a more advanced level, however, Tertullian's ethical teaching, with all its implications, could never be accepted by the leadership in the Church. His exegesis of Scripture, though it avoided the allegorising tendencies of the time, was too crude. His insistence that the end was nigh could be supported only by the example of the Montanists, whose enthusiasm had done great harm to the churches of Asia. His disciplinary injunctions, however admirable in themselves, were illustrated by examples of heroic chastity drawn from

Roman history and religion, an odd source for one so opposed to paganism.

Taken together these things could not fail to disturb and alienate responsible opinion in the Church. By themselves, his devotion to the Paraclete and his dispensational theories might have been overlooked, or even accepted by a large percentage of the faithful. The practical consequences of his radicalism, however, proved too much. It is here that Tertullian came into conflict with the rest of the Church and where ultimately his case was lost to the combined forces of tradition, common sense and expediency.

EPILOGUE

Tertullian's elaborate scheme for an ascetic discipline which would restore the Church to the primaeval sancity of Eden was a failure, but it would be a pity if this fact were allowed to obscure his very great achievement. For although there is little or no evidence that his recommendations were ever put into effect or that his sympathies with such fringe groups as the Montanists ever found an echo in subsequent writers, we must not forget that these defects in his work did not prevent later generations from reading and imitating his style and ideas. Tertullian's achievement in fact has little to do with the ultimate consequences of his holiness scheme. His real and lasting contribution to the development of Christian thought lies at a much deeper level.

Tertullian was the first major Christian writer after the New Testament period to perceive clearly and attempt to put into practice the fact that Christianity was a complete intellectual system independent of pagan philosophy. Its base lay in historically verifiable objective truth. Only Christianity could plausibly claim to be based on an authentic divine revelation accurately transcribed in a book which all could read and obey. The centrality of Scripture in his thought is impossible to overestimate. It was the law-book and charter of the Christian thinker, the infallible guide into all truth. Tertullian did not always live up to this principle, as we have seen. If he had he might have avoided certain serious misconceptions in his anthropology and in his understanding of salvation history. Nevertheless, even in these areas his achievement was sufficiently great to mark him out for all time as one of the seminal thinkers of Christendom.

Of crucial importance for his thought was the practical abolition of any effective distinction between soul and flesh in fallen man. If this had been the only thought he had ever had, it would be enough to show that his mind was substantially independent of pagan cultural assumptions. For what ancient theory imagined anything so astonishing as an indissoluble union of spirit and matter? As Tertullian himself was well aware, this idea was radically different from anything contemporary philosophy had to offer. It is true that he was unable to escape completely from the traces of Hellenistic dualism, and this brought him into serious difficulties when he tried to work out a doctrine of the sanctification of the flesh.

More serious than this, however, and fatal to his cause, was his failure to distinguish between temporal and eternal realities with sufficient clarity. By trying to bring the latter into the world of the former, he landed himself in a predicament from which there was no escape. Try as he might, perfection in a sinful world was an unattainable goal which led him to adopt positions which bore no relation to empirical reality. No doubt parallels to this attitude can be found in Stoicism, which also practised a kind of world-denying asceticism, but it is probably mistaken to attribute Tertullian's ideas to its influence. More likely it was a spiritual dilemma arising from within Christianity which lay behind his theological aberrations.

The late second century was a time of crisis for the Church in different ways. The Apostolic Age and those who remembered it had passed from the scene, and with them had gone the last living link with the historical revelation. From now on the Church would be dependent on spiritual leaders who could discern the mind of Christ in Scripture. As yet there was no real doctrine of episcopal authority to which all Christians would willingly submit, and no effective way of suppressing dissident movements or heretical teachers. There must have been many instances where the loudest voice commanded the greatest following, and it is probably no accident that substantial anti-heretical tracts begin to appear at this time. Those who remained faithful to the apostolic witness knew that the battle for truth would henceforth have to be fought as much within the Christian community as outside it, and their attentions were increasingly diverted in this direction.

At the same time, Christianity was at last beginning to make a serious impression of the Graeco-Roman world. Carl Andresen has shown in his masterly study of Origen's *Contra Celsum* (*Logos und Nomos*, Göttingen, 1954) how the intellectual initiative had passed to the Christians as early as the reign of Marcus Aurelius AD 161–80) and how hard pressed the pagans would henceforth be to counter their arguments. The only serious alternative to Christianity was the universalist creed of the Roman Empire, but at the very moment when its power to attract men was to be most severely tested, it was entering a long period of political and economic crisis which would eventually lead to its downfall.

With the benefit of hindsight we can plot the course of history and trace the final victory of the Christian faith. But to the ordinary believer of the time things must have seemed very different. In the turmoil caused by famine and civil war, men turned to Christianity because it offered them a security which no temporal power possessed. In the blood of Jesus Christ hungry souls found forgiveness for their sins and a new assurance that their Creator cared for them. To the Christian belonged the inestimable privilege of that perfect union with the Divine which the philosophers had sought but not attained. Sanctification was the high calling and the sole pursuit of the true believer. But how could this sanctification be attained? Martyrdom was one obvious answer, but it could not be laid on to order, and the danger of recantation was always present to haunt the weaker brethren. Besides, the end was at hand. Christ might return at any moment to claim his own, and who would then be found worthy to reign with him in the Kingdom of God? Surely it would be those who had not soiled their garments, who had kept themselves separate from the sins of the world. It was this consideration more than any other which pushed Tertullian into a position where he had to embrace perfectionism as the only solution to the pressing demands of sanctification.

Later generations have come to terms in one way or another with the tension between the demands of the gospel and the realities of earthly existence, and in the process have rejected Tertullian's solution as extreme and unworkable. But despite his failure, the fundamental assumptions and methods of his theology have remained a model of scriptural interpretation and dogmatic definition which has stood the test of time and provided one of the principal bases of Christian thought. In so far as this is true, however, it is due exclusively to his fidelity to the Word of God. Those who in our day would remain true to this Word would do well to heed his principles and learn from his mistakes. The way to the future lies not in the rejection of the past, but in its rediscovery and re-presentation to each new generation of believers. Only in this way can the Church hope to remain true to itself and true also to the eternal gospel of her Lord and Saviour Jesus Christ.

NOTES

1. Eusebius, *Hist. eccl.* ii.2.4; iii.20.7; 33.3; v.5.6.

2. Cyprian borrowed extensively from Tertullian in his *De oratione dominica, De bono paenitentiae* and *De habitu virginum.* Novatian used the *Adversus Praxean* when composing his *De trinitate* and Lactantius often alludes to such works as the *Apologeticum*, the *Adversus Praxean* and the *Ad Scapulam.*

3. *Comm. in S. Matt.* v.1: *Tertullianus hinc volumen aptissimum scripserit, sed consequens error hominis detraxit scriptis probabilius auctoritatem.*

4. *Op. cit.* '... *usque ad mediam aetatem presbyter Ecclesiae permansisset, invidia postea et contumeliis clericorum Romanae Ecclesiae, ad Montani dogma delapsus ...*'

5. T. D. Barnes, *Tertullian. A Historical and Literary Survey*, Oxford, 1971, p. 108, lists instances in the *Apologeticum* where Tertullian seems to have borrowed from Justin Martyr, Theophilus, Tatian and Apollinaris. Of course these borrowings are conjectural, although in the case of Justin at least, by no means improbable. Other unacknowledged borrowings from Theophilus, Justin and Irenaeus have been suggested by H. Tränkle, *Q.S.F. Tertulliani Adversus Iudaeos*, Wiesbaden, 1964; G. Quispel, *De bronnen van Tertullianus' Adversus Marcionem*, Leiden, 1943, and most recently by C. Moreschini, '*L'Adversus Marcionem* nell' ambito dell'attività letteraria di Tertulliano', *Ommagio a E. Fraenkel*, 1968, pp. 113 ff.

6. *De haer.* 86: *Tertullianus ergo, sicut scripta eius indicant, animam dicit immortalem quidem, sed eam corpus esse contendit: neque hanc tantum, sed ipsum etiam Deum. Nec tamen hinc haereticus dicitur factus. Posset enim quoquo modo putari ipsam naturam substantiamque divinam corpus vocari ... non ergo ideo est Tertullianus factus haereticus; sed quia transiens ad Cataphrygas ... sua conventicula propagavit.*

7. J. Daniélou, in *Recherches de sciences religieuses* 61, 1973, pp. 254–6.

8. Cf. *Treatise* i.4.2: 'To begin with the senses, 'tis evident these faculties are incapable of giving rise to the notion of the *continu'd* existence of their objects, after they no longer appear to the senses. For that is a contradiction in terms ...' And also (ibid.) i.4.1: '... belief is more properly an act of the sensitive part than of the cogitative part of our nature.'

9. In a letter to Wilhelm von Humboldt, dated 22nd August, 1806.

10. A. Neander, *Antignosticus, Geist des Tertullians*, second edition 1849, English translation 1851, p. 206.

11. 'Gnosticism' as recorded by the ancients was but one obscure sect among many; cf. Augustine, *De haer.* 6.

12. K. Hesselberg, *Tertullians Lehre aus seinen Schriften entwickelt*, Dorpat, 1848.

13. See, e.g., G. Uhlhorn, *Fundamenta Chronologiae Tertullianeae*, Göttingen, 1852; H. Grotemeyer, *Ueber Tertullians Leben und Schriften*, Kempen, 1863; K. G. H. Kellner, 'Ueber Tertullians Abhandlung *De pallio* und das Jahr seines Uebertrittes zum Christentum', *Theologische Quartalschrift* 52, 1870, pp. 547–66; A. Hauck, *Tertullians Leben und Schriften*, Erlangen, 1877; G. N. Bonwetsch, *Die Schriften Tertullians nach der Zeit ihrer Abfassung untersucht*, Bonn, 1878.

14. A. Harnack, 'Zur Chronologie der Schriften Tertullians', *Zeitschrift für Kirchengeschichte* 2, 1878, p. 572.

15. See esp. J. Lortz, 'Vernunft und Offenbarung bei Tertullian', *Der Katholik*, II, 1913, pp. 124–40.

16. S. Schlossmann, 'Tertullian im Lichte der Jurisprudenz', *Zeitschrift für Kirchengeschichte* 27, 1906, pp. 251–75, 407–30; *Praescriptiones und Praescripta Verba*, Leipzig, 1907.

17. H. Koch, 'War Tertullian Priester?', *Historisches Jahrbuch der Görresgesellschaft* 28, 1907, p. 95.

18. B. B. Warfield, *Studies in Tertullian and Augustine*, New York, 1930.

19. See e.g., G. Liquier, *L'Apologétique de Tertullien*, Montauban, 1870; A. Jundt, *Argumenti ratio*, etc., Montauban, 1875; J. Condamin, *De Q.S.F. Tertulliano vexatae religionis patrono*, etc., Lyons, 1877; Mgr Freppel, *Tertullien*, Paris, 1887.

20. W. H. C. Frend, *The Donatist Church*, Oxford, 1952, pp. 333 ff.

21. P. de Labriolle, *La crise montaniste*, Paris, 1913; *Les sources de l'histoire du Montanisme*, Fribourg, 1913.

22. See, e.g., his review of G. Esser, *Wer war Praxeas?*, in *Bulletin d'ancienne littérature et d'archéologie chrétienne* I, 1911, p. 228.

23. C. Guignebert, *Tertullien, études sur ses sentiments à l'égard de l'emprise de la société civile*, Paris, 1901.

24. Op. cit., pp. 282 ff.

25. S. Teeuwen, *Sprachlicher Bedeutungswandel bei Tertullian. Ein Beitrag zum Studium der christlichen Sondersprache*, Paderborn, 1926; also, C. Spicq, '*Hypomonè —Patientia*', *Revue des sciences philologiques* 19, 1930, pp. 95–106; H. Janssen, *Kultur und Sprache*, Nijmegen, 1938; F. de Pauw, 'La justification des traditions non-écrites chez Tertullien', *Ephemerides Theologicae Lovanienses* 19, 1942, pp. 5–46; V. Morel, '*Disciplina*, let mot et l'idée représentée par lui dans les oeuvres de Tertullien, *Revue d'histoire ecclésiastique* 40, 1944–5, pp. 5–46, etc.

26. C. Becker, *Tertullians Apologeticum: Werden und Leistung*, München, 1954.

27. R. Braun, *Deus Christianorum: Recherches sur le vocabulaire doctrinal de Tertullien*, Paris, 1962.

28. He had to make do with a combination of *sermo* and *ratio*, and occasionally *verbum*. Cf. *Adv. Prax.* 5.3; *Apol.* 21.10; 21.17.

29. T. D. Barnes, *Tertullian: A Historical and Literary Study*, Oxford, 1971, p. 1.

CHAPTER 2 (pp. 32–65)

1. *Poenulus*, 1.930 ff.
2. On this subject, see Barnes, op. cit., pp. 13–21.
3. J. Morgan, *The Importance of Tertullian in the Development of Christian Dogma*, London, 1928; A. Beck, *Römisches Recht bei Tertullian und Cyprian*, reprint, Aalen, 1967 (orig. ed. 1930).
4. E.g. D. Michaélidès, *Foi, écriture et tradition, ou les* Praescriptiones *chez Tertullien*, Paris, 1969.
5. J. Stirnimann, *Die* Praescriptio *Tertullians im Lichte des römischen Rechtes und der Theologie*, Freiburg in der Schweiz, 1949.
6. A. d'Alès, 'Tertullien, helléniste', *Revue d'études grecques* 50, 1937, pp. 329–62; R. Braun, 'Tertullien et les poètes latins', *Annales de la Faculté des Lettres et Sciences Humaines de Nice* 2, 1967, pp. 21–33.
7. Op. cit., pp. 199–201.
8. G. Esser, *Die Seelenlehre Tertullians*, Paderborn, 1893.
9. G. Schelowsky, *Der Apologet Tertullianus in seinem Verhältnis zu der griechisch-römischen Philosophie*, Leipzig, 1901.
10. G. Hauschild, *Die rationale Psychologie und Erkenntnistheorie Tertullians*, Leipzig, 1880, p. 17.
11. L. Fuetscher, 'Die natürliche Gotteserkenntnis bei Tertullian', *Zeitschrift für katholische Theologie* 51, 1927, pp. 1–34, 217–51.
12. See J. Moffatt, 'Aristotle and Tertullian', *Journal of Theological Studies* 17, 1916, pp. 170–1; J. H. Waszink, '*Traces of Aristotle's Lost Dialogues in Tertullian*', *Vigiliae Christianae* 1, 1947, pp. 137–49; P. Keseling, 'Aristotelisches bei Tertullian?', *Philosophisches Jahrbuch* 57, 1947, pp. 256–7.
13. A. Festugière, 'La composition et l'esprit du *De anima* de Tertullien', *Revue des sciences philologiques* 33, 1949, pp. 129–61.
14. H. Karpp, *Schrift und Geist bei Tertullian*, Gütersloh, 1955; M. Spanneut, *Le stoïcisme des Pères de l'Englise*, Paris, 1957.
15. G. Lazzati, 'Il *De natura deorum*, fonte del *De testimonio animae* di Tertulliano', in *Atene e Roma* 7, 1939, pp. 153–66; I. Opelt, 'Ciceros Schrift *De natura deorum* bei den lateinischen Kirchenvätern', *Antike und Abendland* 12, 1966, pp. 141–55.
16. J. Lebreton, 'Le désaccord de la foi populaire et de la théologie savante dans l'Eglise chrétienne du troisième siècle', *Revue d'histoire ecclésiastique* 19, 1923, pp. 481–506; 20, 1924, pp. 5–37.
17. G. De Vries, *Bijdrage tot de Psychologie van Tertullianus*, Utrecht, 1929.
18. In fact Tertullian never used the expression; see *De carn. Chr.* 5.4: *credibile est, quia ineptum est*. On the origin of the phrase, see A. Vaccari, '*Credo quia absurdum. Chi l'ha detto?*', *Scritti di erudizione e di filologia* 2, 1958, p. 17, who is inconclusive.
19. G. Bardy, *La conversion au christianisme durant les premiers siècles*, Paris, 1949.
20. A. Labhardt, 'Tertullien et la philosophie, ou la recherche d'une position pure', *Museum Helveticum* 7, 1950, pp. 159–80.

21. R. F. Refoulé, 'Tertullien et la philosophie', *Revue des sciences religieuses* 30, 1956, pp. 42–5.

22. C. Tresmontant, *La métaphysique du christianisme et la naissance de la philosophie chrétienne*, Paris, 1961, p. 626:

> Tertullien, comme l'ensemble des Pères, entend par 'la chair' une substance autre que 'l'âme', contrairement à la terminologie biblique. En défendant 'la chair' contre ses détracteurs gnostiques, Tertullien retrouve une exigence en effet authentiquement inhérente à l'anthropologie chrétienne, laquelle est fondée sur l'anthropologie biblique. Mais, comme la plupart des Pères, Tertullien est prisonnier du schème anthropologique dualiste, au moment même où, au nom des principes métaphysiques du Christianisme, il le combat. Tertullien, comme la plupart des Pères, entend par résurrection de la chair, et résurrection des corps, la résurrection de *quelque chose d'autre que l'âme*. Ce sont *deux* choses, *deux* substances, associées certes, mais distinctes, qui selon Tertullien, doivent ressusciter.

23. See J.-M. Hornus, 'Etude sur la pensée politique de Tertullien', *Revue d'histoire et de philosophie religieuses* 38, 1958, pp. 1–38.

24. E. Isichei, *Political Thinking and Social Experience. Some Christian Interpretations of the Roman Empire from Tertullian to Salvian*, Christchurch, 1964.

25. Cf. J. Daniélou, *The Origins of Latin Christianity*, London, 1977.

26. *Comm. ad Titum* 1.5 (PL 26:194 ff.)

27. W. H. C. Frend, *Martyrdom and Persecution in the Early Church*, Oxford, 1965, p. 334; 'Tertulliano e gli Ebrei', *Rivista di Storia, Lettere, Religione* 4, 1968, pp. 3–10; 'A Note on Tertullian and the Jews', *Studia Patristica* 10, 1970, pp. 291–6.

28. Perpetua is mentioned in the *De anima* 55.4 and Justin Martyr twice, *Adv. Val.* 5.1; *Adv. omn. haer.* 7.1. The latter, however, is unlikely to be genuine. Rutilius, otherwise unknown, is mentioned in *De fuga* 5.3.

29. She died in AD 203 and it has been suggested that Tertullian wrote the account of her martyrdom. This, however, is unlikely since, as Barnes has pointed out (op. cit., p. 265), Tertullian misrepresents the *Passio Perpetuae* in the *De anima*. Also he says nothing about Felicity, Perpetua's companion in death.

30. Frend, *Martyrdom*, op. cit., pp. 304–321, seems to think that Africa was exceptional during this period, in that Christianity was more severely persecuted there than elsewhere. The evidence he adduces for this, however, is vague and insufficient. Tertullian himself records numerous contemporary instances of Roman clemency, cf., e.g., *Ad Scapulam* 3.1; 4.3.

31. The view of C. J. M. J. van Beek, *Passio Sanctarum Perpetuae et Felicitatis* 1936, p. 162. As we have already mentioned, (cf. n. 29), this attribution rests on hypotheses which go beyond what the facts warrant.

32. Cf. H. Delehaye, *Les origines du culte des martyrs*, Bruxelles, 1912, p. 41; but it remained a local, and probably rather unusual phenomenon for some decades. There is no evidence that an active cult of martyrs was in existence anywhere in North Africa during Tertullian's lifetime.

33. This, however, was more apparent in theological and hortatory works

on martyrdom than in the hagiographies, which stress the conviction the martyrs had concerning the True God, and say little or nothing about Christ's suffering on earth. Cf. P. Nagel, *Die Motivierung der Askese in der alten Kirche und der Ursprung des Mönchtums, Texte und Untersuchungen* 95, pp. 5–19; W. Völker, *Das Vollkommenheitsideal des Origenes*, Tübingen, 1931, pp. 215–28, etc.

34. *De fuga* 1.3: *quis est enim exitus persecutionis, quis effectus alius nisi probatio et reprobatio fidei qua suos utique Dominus examinavit?*

35. It was no accident that St John and Perpetua saw only martyrs in their visions of heaven, *De anima* 55.4. The theme is a constant one in second-century literature; see, e.g., Ignatius, *Ad Rom.* 4, quoted by Irenaeus, *Adv. haer.* 5.3, etc. As an example of the power of martyrs' blood, there is a revealing account, preserved by John Chrysostom, *Homil.* xl *in Ep. ad Ephes.* 4 *P.G.* 52, p. 85, where an old man is quoted as saying that a particular sin, probably a schism of some kind, was so bad that not even the blood of martyrdom could wipe it out.

36. Clement stressed the importance of Christian obedience whether or not it led to martyrdom, *Strom.* 7.66 ff.; but such balance was rare in the emotionally charged atmosphere of persecution.

37. R. Murray, *Symbols of Church and Kingdom*, Cambridge, 1975, pp. 14–17.

38. For a detailed criticism, see H. E. W. Turner, *The Pattern of Christian Truth*, London, 1954.

39. B. Lonergan, *The Way to Nicea*, London, 1976, pp. 15–16.

40. *The Works of the Rev. John Wesley*, T. Jackson, ed. London, 1856–7, ii, p. 204; vi, pp. 261, 328; x, p. 47, 50; xi, pp. 485–6. Of these, the last is the most detailed reference. Montanism is also claimed as an ancestor of the modern Pentecostal, or Charismatic, Movement. F. D. Bruner, *A Theology of the Holy Spirit*, Grand Rapids, 1973, pp. 36–7, claims that both movements believed that a new and final age of revelation had come and that doctrinal errors have been due more to careless formulation than to intentional heterodoxy!

41. These were the *Alogoi*, condemned by Irenaeus, *Adv. haer.* iii.11.9.

42. Eusebius, *Hist. eccl.* v.16.18–20. But not everybody agreed, and there were some who queried the fact that Montanus himself was not martyred; ibid., v.16.12.

43. Jerome, *Ep.* 41; Epiphanius, *Panarion* 48, and Sozomen, *Hist. eccl.* 2.32 all refer to it. Frend, op. cit., p. 294, claims that it was still in existence in the reign of Leo III the Isaurian (717–40) and quotes as proof John of Damascus, *Haer.* 49. John may have been right, but his accuracy in such matters is not above reproach. For the epigraphical evidence, which peters out in the fourth century, see W. M. Calder, 'The New Jerusalem of the Montanists', *Byzantion* 6, 1931, pp. 421–5; 'Early Christian Epitaphs from Phrygia', *Anatolian Studies* 5, 1955, pp. 25–38; H. Grégoire, 'Inscriptions montanistes et novatiennes', *Byzantion* 8, 1933, pp. 58–65; 'Épigraphie hérétique et hérésie épigraphique', *Byzantion* 10, 1935, pp. 247–50.

44. For a discussion of this date, see Barnes, op. cit., pp. 46 ff.

45. See, e.g., de Labriolle, op. cit., *La crise montaniste*, pp. 298 ff. He says

that Tertullian received 'un Montanisme d'exportation, systématiquement édulcoré'.

46. *De ieiun.* 1.3; *Adv. Prax.* 1.5. Maximilla is the most shadowy of the three as she appears only in conjunction with the others.

47. De Labriolle, op. cit., p. 359.

48. *De mono.* 16.2 (twice); *De ieiun.* 3.2. It is worth noting that both these treatises have been reckoned to be Montanist.

49. Except in the meaning 'butterfly', where the analogy probably lies in the flimsiness of the creature.

50. Op. cit., p. 356: A dire vrai, même dans ses ouvrages les plus ouvertement montanistes, *nostri* (*nos, nobis,* etc.) n'a pas toujours le sens 'sectaire' et il faut y regarder d'assez près. Ainsi *de vir. vel.* 17.2, par les mots: *nobis Dominus etiam revelationibus velaminis spatia metatus est.* Tertullien ne prétend point distinguer les siens des Catholiques, mais les Catholiques – parmi lesquels il se range – des païens dont il vient d'alléguer les pratiques; *de monog.* 9, le *nobis* s'applique aux chrétiens en général, par contraste avec les *Romani*; *adv. Prax.* 5.5: *in usu est nostrorum per simplicitatem interpretationis 'sermonem' dicere, nostrorum* désigne soit 'nos traducteurs' or 'les nôtres' en général (=nos frères chrétiens), ou encore 'les Latins' par opposition aux *Graeci* que Tertullien vient de nommer; *de pud.* 19.5, on n'ose trop décider si *apud nos* signifie 'chez nous catholiques' ou 'chez nous, montanistes': plutôt cela que ceci, car 1° déjà dans le *de bapt.* 15.6, traité catholique, Tertullien se déclare hostile à la validité du baptême des hérétiques; 2° la même solution devait être adoptée par l'Eglise d'Afrique dans le concile tenu à Carthage, sous Agrippinus, vers 225.

51. D. Powell, 'Tertullianists and Cataphrygians', *Vigiliae Christianae* 29, 1975, pp. 33–54.

52. Cf. *Adv. haer.* v.32 ff.

53. H. von Campenhausen, *The Formation of the Christian Bible,* Eng. trans. London, 1971, pp. 221–6.

54. This has already been substantially claimed by H. Karpp, *Schrift und Geist bei Tertullian,* Gutersloh, 1955, p. 15, and even de Labriolle, op. cit., p. 315, has to admit: ... quelle allégresse pour Tertullien de voir refleurir au sein du Montanisme tous les phénomènes religieux dont l'Ecriture, surtout les Epîtres de S. Paul, lui avait révélé la signification ...'

55. His actual words are: *'quid, si pseudopropheticus spiritus pronuntiavit?'*

56. His opposition to digamy in particular was widespread, shared as it was by Athenagoras, *Supplicatio* 33, Clement of Alexandria, *Strom.* iii. 12.82.4 and Origen, *Hom. in Luc.* 17.

57. This point is made most forcefully in relation to marriage, *De exhort. cast.* 5.2–4.

CHAPTER 3 (pp. 66–94)

1. *De opif. mund.* 69.71.71; *De conf. ling.* 169. Philo much preferred *eikōn* to *homoiōsis*; the latter word occurs no more than six times in his work.

2. On this see esp. T. Ware, *The Orthodox Church,* London, 1963, pp. 224–8.

For a more detailed exposition see V. Lossky, *In the Image and Likeness of God*, London, 1975.

3. *Hom.* 10.4. The dating of the Homilies is uncertain, and it may be better to put them in the third or even in the fourth century, though it is always possible that they reflect genuine Clementine teaching.

4. This was the view put forward by E. Klebba, *Die Anthropologie des heiligen Irenäus*, Münster, 1894.

5. *History of Dogma* II, p. 268.

6. This is implied, e.g. *Adv. Marc.* ii.6.3, where Tertullian insists on coupling *imago* and *similitudo* no fewer than three times in a single paragraph describing man before the fall. It also ties in well with *De bapt.* 5.7.

7. H. Ridderbos, *Paul: An Outline of his Theology*, Grand Rapids, 1975, pp. 57–86. Ridderbos expresses Tertullian's point of view exactly when he says: '... Christ's divine power and glory, already in His pre-existence, are defined in categories that have been derived from His significance as the Second Adam' (p. 73).

8. *Theological Dictionary of the New Testament*, II. p. 397.

9. Unless, of course, the lost treatise, *De censu animae*, can be identified with the *De testimonio animae*, though that is unlikely.

10. The two major works have been G. Esser, *Die Seelenlehre Tertullians*, Paderborn, 1893, and more recently J. H. Waszink's monumental commentary on the *De anima*, Amsterdam, 1947.

11. E.g. A. H. Armstrong, *An Introduction to Ancient Philosophy*, London, 1947, p. 168.

12. On this see J. Dillon, *The Middle Platonists*, London, 1977, p. 82, *et passim*.

13. Tertullian certainly knew of Aristotle's philosophy and argued against it, but that is another question; cf. *De anima* 19.

14. Aristotle, i.659b.17–9; 669a.1; 743b.37 ff., etc. In the *De univ.* i.394b, he says: *legetai de kai heterōs pneuma hē te en phytois kai zōois kai dia pantōn diēkousa empsychos te kai gonimos ousia.* According to Diogenes Laertius, this idea comes originally from Xenophanes (cf. ix.2.3) and Plutarch (*Plac. Phil.* 1.3) ascribes a similar idea to Xenophanes' contemporary Anaximenes.

15. See, e.g., E. De Witt Burton, *Spirit, Soul, Flesh*, Chicago, 1918, pp. 41–8.

16. Thus Dillon, op. cit., p. 143. Of course Philo himself did not look at it this way. As far as he was concerned the Greek philosophers had derived all their best ideas from Moses and were therefore in a sense crypto-Jews.

17. On this see Ware, op. cit., pp. 224 ff.

18. R. Jewett, *Paul's Anthropological Terms*, Leiden, 1971, pp. 448–9.

19. Tertullian never tired of quoting John 1.14, *sermo caro factus est*. There are at least seven instances of it in his writings, *De carn. Chr.* 19.2; 20.3; *Adv. Prax.* 16.6; 21.4; 26.4; *De pud.* 6.16; 16.7.

20. *De resurr. mort.* 50. The argument was that all flesh and blood would be resurrected, but that not all would inherit the kingdom of God, since there was to be a resurrection of judgment also. The flesh of Christians, however, would put on incorruption (1 Cor. 15.53) and *in that state* would inherit the kingdom.

21. For a systematic refutation of Harnack, see J. N. D. Kelly, *Early Christian Creeds*, London, 1952. See also E. W. Kohls' critique of modern hermeneutics in *Theologische Zeitschrift* 26, 1970, pp. 321–37; ibid., 27, 1971, pp. 20–39.

22. Cf., e.g., R. E. Roberts, *The Theology of Tertullian*, London, 1924, p. 180.

23. This idea is first found in *Cyprian*, Ep. 63.14. Tertullian, however, thought of the atonement primarily in relation to baptism, and virtually ignored the eucharist.

24. Though he did not accept that it was a complete satisfaction, cf. *De paen.* 2.4, *et passim*.

25. A point well made by R. A. Norris, *God and World in Early Christian Thought*, London, 1966, pp. 96–103.

26. This point seems to have been missed in recent discussions of the subject; cf., e.g., V. Lossky, op. cit., pp. 71–98, and G. S. Hendry, 'From the Father and the Son: the *Filioque* after Nine Hundred Years', *Theology Today* 11, 1954–5, pp. 449–59.

27. On *theōsis*, cf. V. Lossky, *The Mystical Theology of the Eastern Church*, Cambridge, 1957, pp. 7–43. Lossky and other apologists of Eastern Orthodoxy make much of the development of the Eastern tradition from these primitive roots, but they seldom offer an adequate critique of the Platonic concept of sin underlying it. If that is rejected, however, it is hard to see how the result of the mystical tradition can retain its validity, and its rejection by the Western Church (on the whole) should occasion no surprise.

28. The modern view, defended by Lossky, op. cit., *In the Image* ..., pp. 71–98.

CHAPTER 4 (pp. 95–123)

1. *De vir. vel.* 4. Tertullian rests his case on the argument that *mulier* was a general term for 'woman', including a *virgo*. Strictly speaking, he may have been right, though *mulier* more naturally suggested a woman with sexual experience. Examination of the modern Romance languages shows that it is in the linguistically peripheral areas that the double meaning of 'woman' and 'wife' has been preserved, while the more central areas now restrict the sense to 'wife' – an indication of the weight which must have attached to the word in Latin. Thus in the former category we have Castilian *mujer*, Portuguese *mulher* and Romanian *muiere* (this last being now derogatory) while in the latter are Catalan *muller*, Provençal *molher*, Italian *moglie* and Old French *moillier* (though Modern French *femme* belongs to the first category).

2. On *persona* and *substantia*, see S. Schlossmann, 'Tertullian im Lichte der Jurisprudenz', *Zeitschrift für Kirchengeschichte* 27, 1906, pp. 251–75, 407–30. On the jurist Tertullianus, see T. Barnes, *Tertullian*, Oxford, 1971, pp. 22–9.

3. Cf. *Adv. Iud.* 2.9; 3.7; 6.2. Also, *De mono.* 7.4.

4. B. Capelle, 'Le symbole romain au second siècle', *Revue bénédictine* 39, 1928, p. 38.

5. J. M. Restrepo-Jaramillo, 'Tertuliano y la doble fórmula en el símbolo apostólico', *Gregorianum* 15, 1934, pp. 56–8.

6. V. Morel, 'Le développement de la *disciplina* sous l'action du Saint-Esprit chez Tertullien', *Revue d'Histoire ecclésiastique* 35, 1939, pp. 243–65.

7. The third occurrence of the *regula* which Morel does not cite in this context, comes in *Adv. Prax.* 2.1. It is, on the whole, closer to the form of *De vir. vel.*, but with the important addition of a clause explaining the role of the Holy Spirit as Paraclete.

8. See H. von Campenhausen, *The Formation of the Christian Bible*, Eng. trans. London, 1972 (German edition, 1968), pp. 274–5.

9. P. Stein, *Regulae Iuris*, Edinburgh, 1966, pp. 49–73.

10. In *Ad Plautium* xvi, cited by P. Stein, op. cit., p. 67.

11. N. Cohn, *The Pursuit of the Millennium*, pp. 108–9.

12. This is a point which seems to have been missed even by J. Moingt, *La théologie trinitaire de Tertullien*, 4 vols, Paris, 1966–9.

13. This may be inferred from several facts. (1) He is fond of repeating the phrase *lex et prophetae usque ad Iohannem* (Matt. 11.13) which occurs eight times in his writings. (2) He is insistent that John's mission was to announce the coming Messiah, a task which he performed by baptising men for the remission of sins, cf. *De bapt.* 10.5 ff. (3) Christ himself underwent John's baptism, when the Spirit of God descended on him, *De carn. Chr.* 3.8. (4) The crucifixion did not supersede the baptism but confirmed it. Not only did Pilate wash his hands in water to excuse himself from responsibility, but water even flowed from the pierced side of the Saviour, *De bapt.* 9.4.

14. The phrase was particularly important to him because it signified the end of the period of God's initial indulgence towards man. The abolition of the Law meant only that sin, which the Law had restrained, was now to be wiped out entirely. This is made clear, e.g., in *De pud.* 6.2.

15. This has been the case, for example, in the recently revived Pentecostal (Charismatic) Movement. For a discussion of this, see F. D. Bruner, *A Theology of the Holy Spirit*, Grand Rapids, 1970, pp. 36–7.

16. *De anima* 9.4. The famous case of the woman who had visions in Church has often, though not always, been held to be an example of Montanism. The main supporting evidence for this seems to be that only Montanists would allow women to prophesy. But this is not so. Philip the Evangelist had four daughters who were prophetesses (Acts 21.8) and although St Paul specifically forbade women to teach or to preach, he never denied them the right to prophesy. Tertullian followed the Apostle faithfully, even after coming into contact with the Montanists; cf., e.g., *De vir. vel.* 9.1.

17. John 16.7. The word also had a wide circulation in heretical Judaism, but there is no indication that Tertullian, or the Montanists for that matter, got their term from that source. Cf. O. Betz, *Der Paraklet*, Leiden, 1963.

18. See S. Otto, *Natura und dispositio. Eine Untersuchung zum Naturbegriff und zur Denkform Tertullians*, München, 1960.

19. Op. cit., p. 264:

... dans l'évolution de la *disciplina*, l'auteur accorde une importance primordiale à la *ratio,* c'est-à-dire, au fondement rationnel des traditions et des pratiques extra-scripturaires. Dans cette perspective, il est naturel qu'une institution humaine, qui s'est révélée conforme à la raison et utile au bien des âmes (la constitution hiérarchique de l'Eglise) soit un jour confirmée par le Paraclet et, d'institution humaine qu'elle était, élevée au rang d'institution divine ...

20. F. De Pauw, 'La justification des traditions non-écrites chez Tertullien', *Ephemerides Theologicae Lovanienses* 19, 1942, p. 11; R. P. C. Hanson, *Origen's Doctrine of Tradition,* London, 1954, pp. 189–90.

21. J. Fontaine, *De corona,* Paris, 1966.

22. J. Ellul, *The Theological Foundation of Law,* New York, 1960, p. 25.

23. Cf. *Adv. Marc.* iii.20.10. On the subject of *ratio* and its meaning in Tertullian, see G. Bray, 'The Legal Aspect of *Ratio* in Tertullian', *Vigiliae Christianae* 31, 1977, pp. 94–116.

24. Fr. B3.ii.264.23 (Diels): *physeōs kai askēseōs didaskalia deitai.*

25. Fr. B33.ii.153.1 (Diels): *hē physis kai hē didachē.*

26. Cf. O. Du Roy, *L'intelligence de la foi en la Trinité selon Saint Augustin,* Paris, 1966, pp. 299–303; also P. Hadot, 'Etre, vie, pensée chez Plotin et avant Plotin', *Recherches sur l'antiquité classique* V : *Les sources de Plotin,* Vandoeuvres-Genève, 1957, pp. 107–57 (esp. pp. 123–9).

27. Quoted in Menan. Siob., p. 240: *omnia fiunt tribus causis nomōi anakēi ethei tini.*

28. The formula with *mathēsis* is found in Philo (Cohn-Wendland) as follows: ii.13.17; iii.241.8; iv.61.4; v.350.16:

With *didaskalia:* iii.79.14; iv.13.3; iv.13.8; v.347.7.

In iii.240.20 Philo puts *mathēsis* at the end: *tēn aretēn ē physei ē askēsei ē mathēsei;* and once (iii.158.2) he speak of the three *physeis,* replacing *physus* in the triad by *teleiotēs: tōn triōn physeōn didaskalias teleiotētos askēseōs.*

29. In addition to the example quoted in n. 28, there is only one other exception to this in Philo, *De Abrahamo* 54. Du Roy, op. cit., p. 301, n. 2 gives two examples, but the first of these is incorrect. Following Hadot, du Roy recognises that the three elements of the triad are interdependent, but he does not examine the significance attached to the order in which they appear.

30. Cf., e.g., *De praescr. haer.* 44.5, which refers to Rom. 16.17 and *Adv. Marc.* iv.13.1, which is a translation of Mark 1.22 (Matt. 7.29; Luke 4.32).

31. V. Morel, '*Disciplina,* le mot et l'idée représentée par lui dans les oeuvres de Tertullien', *Revue d'histoire ecclésiastique* 40, 1944–5, pp. 5–46. See also H. Marrou, '*Doctrina* et *disciplina* dans la langue des Pères de l'Eglise', *Archivum latinitatis medii aevi* 9, 1934, p. 5. Of lesser interest is W. Dürig, '*Disciplina.* Eine Studie zum Bedeutungsumfang des Wortes in der Sprache der Liturgie under Väter', *Sacris Erudiri* 4, 1952, pp. 245–79.

32. E.g. Heb. 12.5 (Prov. 3.11). Tertullian used *disciplina* in *Adv. Marc.* v.18.11 to translate *paideia* in Eph. 6.4.

33. Of course, *paideia* in the New Testament did not mean what it meant to classical educators, whatever Morel (op. cit., pp. 27 ff.) may think. This *paideia* was rendered in Latin by *humanitas;* cf. Aulus Gellius xiii.16.1. See

also H. I. Marrou, *St Augustin et la fin de la culture antique*, Paris, 1938, pp. 552–4, where he cites P. de Labriolle, 'Pour l'histoire du mot *humanitas*', *Les humanités, Classes de lettres* VIII, 1931–2, pp. 478–9.

34. Morel, for example, speaks, op. cit., p. 44, of: ... l'ascétisme vigoureux et impitoyable d'un Tertullien ...; but he nowhere mentions *askēsis*.

35. This would certainly accord well with Tertullian's use of Scripture and his style of exegesis; cf. Moingt, op. cit., I, pp. 177–82; also T. P. O'Malley, *Tertullian and the Bible. Language, Imagery, Exegesis*, Nijmegen, 1967.

CHAPTER 5 (pp. 124–152)

1. Cf., e.g., *Gospel of Thomas* 114.
2. Eusebius actually believed that Philo was referring to Christians under another name; cf. *Hist. eccl.* ii.17.18–19.
3. R. Murray, *Symbols of Church and Kingdom*, Cambridge, 1975, pp. 11–12.
4. A. Vööbus, *History of Asceticism in the Syrian Orient*, Vol. I, Louvain, 1958, pp. 45–61.
5. Eusebius, op. cit., iv.30.
6. It seems that even Bishop Anicetus (d. 172) was of Syrian extraction, and there must have been many orientals at Rome long before this. Juvenal speaks of the 'scum of the Orontes' (the river of Antioch) flowing into the Tiber, which indicates that there was a flourishing Syrian community at Rome a generation or two before this date.
7. Epiphanius, *Panarion* 46.1 says that Tatian returned to the East in the twelfth year of Antoninus Pius, which would place it in AD 150. But this cannot be right. Epiphanius has confused Antoninus with his adopted son Marcus Aurelius (reigned 161–80).
8. Vööbus, op. cit., p. 41.
9. Ibid., p. 36.
10. Cf. Gen. 38.21; 1 Kgs. 22.47; 2 Kgs. 23.7; Hos. 4.14; Job 36.14.
11. Barnes, op. cit., pp. 13–21.
12. Irenaeus, *Adv. haer.* iii.23.8, claims that Tatian even denied salvation to Adam because he had known his wife. Tertullian, however, fully approved of marriage and procreation under the old dispensation; see, e.g., *De mono.* 7.3; *De pud.* 16.19.
13. This requires some explanation. Daniélou, whose theories are discussed here, tried to claim a common Judaeo-Christian parentage for both Syrian and Latin Christianity. The idea that Montanism may also have developed under Judaic influence has been put forward by J. M. Ford, 'Was Montanism a Jewish–Christian Heresy?', *Journal of Ecclesiastical History* 17, 1966, pp. 145–58. It should be said, however, that her views are exceptionally ingenious and have commanded no support.
14. J. G. Daniélou, *A History of Early Christian Doctrine before the Council of Nicaea*, Volume 1: *The Theology of Jewish Christianity*, London, 1964, and Volume 3: *The Origins of Latin Christianity*, London, 1977.
15. Ibid., Vol. 3, pp. 17–98.
16. Ibid., Vol. 3, p. 38.

17. Tertullian realised that Latin *homo-humus* (ground) paralleled the Hebrew *'āḏām-'ᵃḏāmâh* (cf. *Apol.* 18.1; *Adv. Marc.* v.10.9) but ignored the even more striking connection between *femina* and *femur* (thigh) with its suggestion that woman was created from a human bone. He may have failed to perceive this, however, since by his day the ancient declension (*feminis*, etc.) had been reconstructed (*femoris*, etc.), and even Augustine makes no mention of it.

18. E. Williger, Hagios – *Untersuchungen zur Terminologie des Heiligen in den hellenisch-hellenistischen Religionen*, Giessen, 1922.

19. Murray, op. cit., pp. 14 ff.

20. Vööbus, op. cit., pp. 78–83.

21. It is generally thought that his wife died before the later treatises on marriage were written, which would explain why she is not mentioned in them. But this is an argument from silence, and may not be correct.

22. But see *De mono.* 5.5, where Tertullian denied that Adam was married before the Fall. Probably what he meant was that Adam had not had sexual relations with his wife.

23. *De mono.* 9. The texts he used to defend matrimony were Matt. 5.32, 19.6; Gen. 2.23. His repudiation of divorce, it should be noted, was based on eschatological, rather than ethical or moral considerations.

24. *De pud.* 1.6. His identity is disputed, some preferring Zephyrinus, others Callistus. Barnes, op. cit., p. 247, argues that the *episcopus episcoporum* was an unknown bishop of Carthage, but this is most improbable, since Tertullian also called him *pontifex maximus*, an obviously Roman title.

25. On the development of *koinē*, see R. Browning, *Mediaeval and Modern Greek*, London, 1969. Oddly enough, the perfect subjunctive in Latin could also have the force of a Greek aorist, and thus denote future time. This usage, however, had probably passed out of currency by Tertullian's time.

26. Ibid., 7.1. This 'quotation' is from Lev. 21.13–4, which Tertullian read as *sacerdotes ne plus nubent*.

27. See G. Zimmermann, *Die hermeneutischen Prinzipien Tertullians*, Würzburg, 1937.

28. See Jerome, *De vir. ill.* 53; *Comm. in Ep. ad Titum* 1.6; also Augustine, *De bono vid.* 4.6.

29. On this subject, see J. Lebreton, 'Le désaccord de la foi populaire et de la théologie savante dans l'église chrétienne du troisième siècle', *Revue de l'histoire ecclésiastique* 19, 1923, pp. 481–506; ibid., 20, 1924, pp. 5–37.

LIST OF
TERTULLIAN'S WORKS

These are given in the order in which they appear in the *Corpus Christianorum, Series Latina*, Turnhout, 1954. The arrangement is roughly chronological, in so far as an order can be determined. The fifth book of the *Adversus Marcionem* and subsequent works are generally held to exhibit Montanist influence. English equivalents for the Latin titles are given in brackets, but these do not necessarily correspond to forms actually in use.

1. *Ad martyras* (To the Martyrs)
2. *Ad nationes* (To the Gentiles)
3. *Apologeticum* (Apology)
4. *De testimonio animae* (On the Witness of the Soul)
5. *De praescriptione haereticorum* (On the Prescription of Heretics)
6. *De spectaculis* (On Spectacles)
7. *De oratione* (On Prayer)
8. *De baptismo* (On Baptism)
9. *De patientia* (On Suffering)
10. *De paenitentia* (On Repentance)
11. *De cultu feminarum* (On Women's Apparel)
12. *Ad uxorem* (To his Wife)
13. *Adversus Hermogenem* (Against Hermogenes)
14. *Adversus Marcionem* (Against Marcion)
15. *De pallio* (On the Cloak)
16. *Adversus Valentinianos* (Against the Valentinians)
17. *De anima* (On the Soul)
18. *De carne Christi* (On the Flesh of Christ)
19. *De resurrectione mortuorum* (On the Resurrection of the Dead)
20. *De exhortatione castitatis* (An Exhortation to Chastity)
21. *De corona* (On the Soldier's Crown)
22. *Scorpiace* (The Scorpion)
23. *De idololatria* (On Idolatry)
24. *Ad Scapulam* (To Scapula)
25. *De fuga in persecutione* (On Flight from Persecution)
26. *Adversus Praxean* (Against Praxeas)
27. *De virginibus velandis* (On the Veiling of Virgins)
28. *De monogamia* (On Monogamy)
29. *De ieiunio adversus Psychicos* (On Fasting – against the Psychici)
30. *De pudicitia* (On Modesty)
*31. *De fato.* (On Fate)

* only fragments survive

*32. *Adversus Apelleiacos*   (Against the Apelleians)
*33. *De extasi*   (On Ecstasy)
**34. *Adversus Iudaeos*   (Against the Jews)
**35. *Adversus omnes haereses*   (Against All Heresies)

 * only fragments survive
** works of doubtful authenticity

English translations of Tertullian's writings are usually to be found as parts of a series, of which the three volumes dedicated to him in the *Anti-Nicene Christian Library* (Edinburgh 1869–70) remain the best known. More recently, the Catholic University of Washington, D.C., has sponsored a new series, *The Fathers of the Church* (New York, 1959–), in which his works also appear. Individual treatises occasionally come out in bilingual editions, the most significant recent contribution being E. F. Evans' edition and translation of the *Adversus Marcionem* (2 vols), Oxford, 1972.

BIBLIOGRAPHY

All quotations from the text of Tetullian's works, and references to them, are taken from the composite edition of the *Corpus Christianorum, Series Latina,* Turnhout, 1954.

Alaja, Osmo, *Piirteita Tertullianuksen pyhityskäsitysestä,* Helsinki, 1944.

Aland, Kurt, 'Bemerkungen zum Montanismus und zur frühchristlichen Eschatologie', *Kirchengeschichtliche Entwürfe,* 1960, p. 105.

—— 'Der Montanismus und die kleinasiatische Theologie', *Zeitschrift für die Neutestamentliche Wissenschaft,* 46, 1955, pp. 109–16.

Barnes, Timothy D., *Tertullian. A Historical and Literary Study,* Oxford, 1971.

Bauer, Walter, *Orthodoxy and Heresy in Earliest Christianity,* London, 1972 (first German edition, Tübingen, 1934).

Beck, Alexander, 'Römisches Recht bei Tertullian und Cyprian', *Schriften der Königsberger gelehrten Gesellschaft,* Geisteswiss, K. 7.2, 1930.

Becker, Carl, *Tertullians* Apologeticum. *Werden und Leistung,* München, 1954.

Bender, Wolfgang, *Die Lehre über den heiligen Geist bei Tertullian,* München, 1961.

Braun, René, Deus Christianorum. *Recherches sur le vocabulaire doctrinal de Tertullien,* Paris, 1962.

Campenhausen, Hans, *Die Idee des Martyriums in der alten Kirche,* Göttingen, 1936.

—— *The Formation of the Christian Bible,* London, 1972 (German edition, Göttingen, 1968).

Courcelle, Pierre, 'Deux grands courants de pensée dans la littérature latine tardive: stoicisme et néoplatonisme', *Revue d'études latines,* 42, 1964, pp. 122–40.

Daniélou, Jean, *The Origins of Latin Christianity,* London, 1977.

Dodds, Eric, *Pagan and Christian in an Age of Anxiety,* Cambridge, 1965.

Dürig, Walter, *Disciplina.* 'Eine Studie zum Bedeutungsumfang des Wortes in der Sprache der Liturgie und der Väter', *Sacris Erudiri* 4, 1952, pp. 245–79.

Edelstein, Ludwig, *The Idea of Progress in Classical Antiquity,* Baltimore, 1967.

Ellspermann, G. L., *The Attitude of the Early Christian Latin Writers toward Pagan Literature and Learning,* Washington, 1949.

Esser, Gerhard, *Die Seelenlehre Tertullians,* Paderborn, 1893.

Faggiotto, Agostino, 'La diasporà catafrigia: Tertulliano e la "Nuova Profezia"', *Collezione* GRAPHE 4, 1924.

Flesseman-van Leer, Ellen, *Tradition and Scripture in the Early Church,* Assen, 1953.

Fontaine, Jacques, *Aspects et problèmes de la prose d'art latine au troisième siècle*, Torino, 1968.

—— 'Permanencia y mutaciones de los géneros literarios clásicos de Tertuliano a Lactancio', *Actas del tercer congreso espanol de estudios clasicos*, Madrid, 1968, pp. 126–36.

Fredouille, Jean-Claude, *Tertullien et la conversion de la culture antique*, Paris, 1972.

Frend, W. H. C., *The Donatist Church*, Oxford, 1952.

—— *Martyrdom and Persecution in the Early Church*, Oxford, 1965.

Hanson, R. P. C., 'Notes on Tertullian's Interpretation of Scripture', *Journal of Theological Studies*, n.s. 12, 1961, pp. 273–9.

Harnack, Adolf von, *A History of Dogma*, London, 1895 (German edition, Giessen, 1885).

—— *Marcion. Das Evangelium vom fremden Gott*, Leipzig, 1902.

Hesselberg, Karl, *Tertullians Lehre aus seinen Schriften entwickelt*, Dorpat, 1848.

Karpp, Heinrich, *Schrift und Geist bei Tertullian*, Gütersloh, 1955.

Klein, Richard, *Tertullian und das römische Reich*, Heidelberg, 1968.

Labriolle, Pierre de, *La crise montaniste*, Paris, 1913.

—— *Les sources de l'histoire du montanisme*, Fribourg, 1913.

Lortz, Joseph, *Tertullian als Apologet*, Münster, 1927.

Maistre, A. P., '*Traditio*. Aspects théologiques d'un terme de droit chez Tertullien', *Revue des sciences philologiques* 51, 1967, pp. 617–43.

Moingt, Joseph, *La théologie trinitaire de Tertullien*, Paris 1966–9.

Monceaux, Paul, *Histoire littéraire de l'Afrique chrétienne*, vol. 1: *Tertullien et les origines*, Paris, 1901.

Morel, Valentin, 'Le développement de la *disciplina* sous l'action du Saint-Esprit chez Tertullien', *Revue d'histoire ecclésiastique* 35, 1939, pp. 243–65.

—— '*Disciplina*, le mot et l'idée représentée par lui dans les oeuvres de Tertullien', *Revue d'histoire ecclésiastique* 40, 1944–5, pp. 5–46.

Neander, August, *Antignosticus. Geist des Tertullians*, 1825.

Noeldechen, Ernst, *Tertullian dargestellt*, Gotha, 1890.

O'Malley, T. P., *Tertullian and the Bible. Language, Imagery, Exegesis*, Nijmegen, 1967.

Pauw, Frans de, 'La justification des traditions non-écrites chez Tertullien', *Ephemerides Theologicae Lovanienses* 19, 1942, pp. 5–46.

Powell, Douglas, 'Tertullianistae and Cataphrygians', *Vigiliae Christianae* 29, 1975, pp. 33–54.

Rausch, Gotthard, *Der Einfluss der stoischen Philosophie auf die Lehrbildung Tertullians*, Halle, 1890.

Refoulé, François, 'Tertullien et la philosophie', *Revue des sciences religieuses* 30, 1956, pp. 42–5.

Restrepo-Jaramillo, José-Maria, 'Tertuliano y la doble fórmula en el símbolo apostólico', *Gregorianum* 15, 1934, pp. 3–58.

Rivet, Denise, *Tertullien et l'écriture*, Lyon, 1958.

Roberts, Robert, *The Theology of Tertullian*, London, 1924.

Schelowsky, George, *Der Apologet Tertullianus in seinem Verhältnis zu der griechisch-römischen Philosophie*, Leipzig, 1901.

Shortt, C. De Lisle, *The Influence of Philosophy on the Mind of Tertullian*, London, 1933.

Spanneut, Michel, *Le stoicisme des Pères de l'Eglise de Clément de Rome à Clément d'Alexandrie*, Paris, 1957.

—— *Tertullien et les premiers moralistes africains*, Paris, 1969.

Teeuwen, Stephan, *Sprachlicher Bedeutungswandel bei Tertullian. Ein Beitrag zum Studium der christlichen Sondersprache*, Paderborn, 1926.

Tibiletti, Carlo, 'Verginità e matrimonio in antichi scrittori cristiani', *Annali della Facoltà di Lettere e Filosofia dell'Università di Macerata* 2, 1969, pp. 9–217.

Tresmontant, Claude, *La métaphysique du christianisme et al naissance de la philosophie chrétienne*, Paris, 1961.

Vecchiotti, Icilio, *La filosofia di Tertulliano. Un colpo di sonda nella storia del cristianesimo primitivo*, Urbino, 1970.

Vellico, Antonio, *La rivelazione e le sue fonti nel* De praescrptione haereticorum *di Tertulliano. Studio storico-dogmatico*, Roma, 1935.

Vitton, Paolo, *I concetti giurdici nelle opere di Tertulliano*, Roma, 1924.

Vööbus, Arthur, *A History of Asceticism in the Syrian Orient*, Louvain, 1958–60.

Vries, G. J. de, *Bijdrage tot de psychologie van Tertullianus*, Utrecht, 1929.

Williger, Eduard, Hagios, —*Untersuchungen zur Terminologie des Heiligen in den hellenisch-hellenistischen Religionen*, Giessen, 1922.

Zimmermann, Gottfried, *Die hermeneutischen Prinzipien Tertullians*, Würzburg, 1937.

INDEX OF PERSONAL NAMES

A. ANCIENT AND MEDIAEVAL

B. MODERN

INDEX OF SUBJECTS

WORD LISTS

A. HEBREW

'ād̲ām-'ᵃd̲āmàh, 168n.
mûsār, 122
qᵉdēšàh, 139

B. SYRIAC

bethul/-a, -ta, -uta, 127, 140, 141
ihiday/ -a, -uta, 128, 129, 131, 142
qaddish/-in, -uta, 128, 140, 142

C. GREEK

anakephalaiōsis, 71
anankē, 119, 150
aphrodisiastika, 138
askēsis, 117, 119, 121, 122
charisma, 115
didachē, 117, 121, 122
didaskalia, 121
eikōn, 67, 72
epainos, 117
epimeleia, 117
epithymētikon, 76, 78
eschaton, 150
ethos, 117, 118
gnōsis, 58
graphē, 51
gynē, 96
hagios, 138, 139
hagneutika, 138
hagnizein, 138
hagnos, 137–139
hēgemonikon, 76
homoiōsis, 67, 72
kanōn, 102
katharos, 137–139
kosmos, 76, 96
logikon, logistikon, 76
logos, 28, 77, 117, 119
mathēsis, 117–121
monachos, 128
monogenēs, 128
noētikē, 77
nomos, 117–120
nous, 77
paideia, 121–122
parousia, 124, 140, 149, 150
philosophia, 117
physis, 112, 117–121
pneuma, 77, 82
pneumatikos, 57 58
pnoē, 69, 74
psychē, 58, 77, 81, 82
psychikos, 57, 58, 82
sarkikos, sarkinos, 82
symphyton pneuma, 77
theōsis, 89
thymikon, thymoeides, 76, 78
thymos, 76

D. LATIN

anima, 58
animalis, 57, 58, 82
ars, 118–120
carnalis, 53, 82, 83
castitas, castus, 134–139
consuetudo, 116
corpus, 85
correctio, 122
dignitas, 45
disciplina, 111–122
dispositiones, 105
doctrina, 118, 119, 122
ereptum, 102
femina, 168n.
femur, 168n.
fides, 116
flatus, 69, 74
homo, 168n.
humus, 168n.
imago, 67
imitatio, 83
indulgentia, 109, 143, 147, 149
ingenium, 118–120
institutum, 41–42
lex, 101, 106, 114, 119, 120
lex tingendi, 97
mos, 118–121
natura, 111–122
nos, nostri, 58, 59
Paracletus, 57, 108
persona, 19, 27, 97
psychicus, 57, 59, 60, 82, 83, 107, 144–148
purus, 137, 139
ratio, 113–116
receptum, 102